Injustice in Perugia

a book detailing the wrongful conviction of Amanda Knox and Raffaele Sollecito

Bruce Fisher

To my beautiful wife and three amazing children for their patience and unwavering support.

Contents

For all those who have been wrongfully convicted.

Preface

Meredith Kercher was murdered in Perugia, Italy, November 1st, 2007. Meredith was a beautiful young woman who had her life stolen from her in an act of pure evil. Her murder would change many lives forever. For Amanda Knox and Raffaele Sollecito, it was the beginning of a long, drawn-out nightmare that continues to this day.

Three people have been tried and convicted for Meredith Kercher's murder: Rudy Guede, Raffaele Sollecito and Amanda Knox. All credible evidence in this case points to Rudy Guede. Amanda Knox and Raffaele Sollecito had nothing to do with this crime. I will show in great detail that Amanda Knox and Raffaele Sollecito have been wrongfully convicted.

Was this a rush to judgment by the local authorities, or was the cause of this injustice the result of something far more corrupt?

Many details have already been written about this case. I will provide a brief summary leading up to the murder of Meredith Kercher, but my main focus will be to highlight the events that led to the wrongful conviction of Amanda Knox and Raffaele Sollecito. If you would like to read a far more detailed account of the people and places along with wonderful insight on Italian culture, I highly recommend that you read *Murder in Italy* by Candace Dempsey. Candace does a wonderful job of bringing the reader to Perugia and providing a true sense of how the days played out for those involved.

With my focus on the wrongful convictions, I will undoubtedly be accused by some of being disrespectful to Meredith Kercher. I truly believe that it shows no disrespect to Meredith to expose the truth. Correcting this injustice to assure that the right person bears full responsibility for her murder is a sign of respect to Meredith. Imprisoning two innocent people will bring no peace and, certainly, no justice for Meredith Kercher.

Why did I get involved?
When I first heard the news of the brutal murder of Meredith Kercher I felt angry and disgusted. Sure, there are murders reported every single day and most of us become jaded to the nightly news, but this case was one that grabbed my attention more than most. This was one of those cases that gave me pause and led me to think about my own family. I thought about my daughter and could not possibly imagine the pain Meredith's parents

must have felt upon hearing this unbearable news. My reaction was certainly not unique. I know many parents think about their own children when they hear about cases like this one. As the days went by and information about Amanda Knox continued to flood the news cycle, I figured that Amanda Knox and Raffaele Sollecito were most likely guilty. After all, the evidence must have been overwhelming for the media to attack the two of them so viciously. I figured the authorities were simply holding the evidence until trial. The one thing that struck me in the beginning was a photograph that circulated showing Amanda and Raffaele standing outside the murder scene. The media kept flashing that photograph, usually placing more focus on Amanda than Raffaele. From the media's description, I was supposed to see Amanda as a sex-crazed murderer. What I saw was a scared young woman who looked as though she were in shock. I put that thought on hold because, after all, the media was bombarding me with information telling me these two people were guilty; but my thoughts of that photograph never left my mind completely. The media continued to be relentless. We have all heard the stories about mop buckets, bleach receipts, Harry Potter books, cartwheels, and let's not forget about the underwear and wild sex. Reports of hard evidence against the two would also be heard. Talk of footprints in blood and Raffaele's DNA on Meredith's bra clasp would paint Amanda and Raffaele as vicious killers. Most importantly, we heard about the key piece of evidence, the "smoking gun" for the prosecution.

They had the murder weapon: the double DNA knife. At that point, for many people, Amanda and Raffaele were guilty. There was no looking back—case closed.

For me, something just was not right about this case. I could not stop thinking about that photograph. Every time I focused in on that image, I saw a young woman who was scared and in shock. I also thought about the fact that Amanda voluntarily went to the police department day after day to talk with investigators about the murder. She could have left, but she stayed. She told her mother on the phone that she wanted to help the police solve the murder. These did not appear to be actions of a guilty person, but again, I put those feelings on hold.

I started to question the case. I started to open up my mind to every aspect of the case. Most of the information the media said in the beginning was turning out to be lies and misinformation. Accusations of leaks by the prosecution were being reported. When the trial started, months went by with no real evidence, just elaborate fantasies from the prosecution and character assassinations of the worst degree. We were all waiting for the evidence that never came. A closer look at the footprints revealed that they were not made in blood; the knife had no blood on the blade; and most importantly, there was no reliable evidence that there was any DNA from Meredith on the knife at all. The knife was randomly taken from a kitchen drawer. No other knives were tested. A spoon could have been taken from the same kitchen and yielded the same result. However, it would have been very hard to claim that Meredith was killed with a spoon. The prosecution had no murder weapon. A closer look at the bra clasp revealed poor evidence handling, and DNA from several other people was found on the clasp, proving it was contaminated. The defense asked for an independent review of the DNA and was denied by the Judge who, by the way, was also a member of the jury. Was his mind already made up? The interrogation of Amanda Knox was ruled inadmissible by the Italian Supreme Court, but the civil trial was running concurrently with the murder trial, so the jury heard the results of the illegal interrogation anyway.

When the limited evidence that was presented by the prosecution was disproved, all that was left to convict Amanda and Raffaele was a cartwheel; but it was too late, the jury slept and the Judge took phone calls.

On the day of the verdict, I knew what the Judge was going to say before he said it. Amanda and Raffaele were two people I had never met, so I was honestly surprised to feel emotions I would normally reserve for family and close friends. I imagined my own daughter in that situation and could not imagine how difficult it must have been for Amanda and Raffaele's parents to witness this injustice being committed to their own children.

At that point in time, I knew I needed to do something to help. I decided to put together a website detailing this injustice. The website has helped to bring together an excellent group of people including various experts that have all worked very hard to provide the information that has been made available on Injusticeinperugia.org. I decided to write this book so that I could continue my efforts of informing as many people as possible about this injustice.

You will find no sensationalized story lines. No efforts have been made to exaggerate any information just for the sake of generating sales. This book was not fun to write, and I honestly wish it was completely unnecessary. I did not write this book for any monetary gain. All net profits from this book will be donated to the Amanda Knox Defense Fund. I am not directly associated with Amanda's family in any way and her family had absolutely nothing to do with the writing of this book. As we all know, defending yourself in a court of law is very expensive. Unfortunately, the court system moves very slowly in Italy. Attorney fees and travel expenses, due to this extended period of time, have taken a huge financial toll on Amanda' family. I am simply doing what I can to help.

When I sat down to write this book, I had one objective in mind, and that objective was to provide the honest truth about this case. I believe the truth is clear for anyone who is willing to see it. Two college students have been wrongfully convicted of murder and are currently sitting in prison. I have done extensive research on this case, including reading independent scientist's opinions regarding DNA evidence, viewing hours of crime scene video, looking at hundreds of photographs and analyzing presentations given by both sides in court. Other references include the court's motivation document, appeals filed by both defense teams, Amanda's e-mail home, and diary excerpts from both Amanda and Raffaele. I am not an expert in any specific field, and I do not pretend to be one. The opinions provided in this book detailing the physical evidence are based on expert opinion from contributors to Injustice in Perugia, along with actual expert testimony that was presented in court. When you look at the facts of this case, it does not take an expert to see that an injustice has occurred.

I am convinced that Amanda and Raffaele are innocent. In fact, I have never been more sure of anything in my life. This was a horrible murder, but not a complicated one. Rudy Guede attacked and murdered Meredith Kercher, and he acted alone. This case became complicated when two innocent people were accused and convicted of murder. Wrongful convictions create additional victims. Amanda and Raffaele are victims. They have been incarcerated for a crime they did not commit. They have gained unwanted fame from this injustice that they must deal with for the rest of their lives. Even if this injustice is corrected on appeal and both Amanda and Raffaele are fully exonerated, there will be no winners in this case. Unfortunately, the damage has already been done. Everyone loses.

1

The Murder of Meredith Kercher

The location of this ongoing nightmare is Perugia, Italy. Perugia is a college town with a student population that now reaches upwards of 40,000, with a total population of about 160,000.

Meredith Kercher came to Perugia from England to attend college at the University of Perugia. The University attracts students from all over the world. Meredith was in her third year of studies at the University of Leeds. She entered a student exchange program and arrived in Italy in August 2007. Meredith quickly met up with other British students studying in Perugia and she began to settle into her new life in Italy.

Meredith shared a hilltop flat, often referred to as a cottage, with another college student, Amanda Knox, and two other women, Filomena Romanelli and Laura Mezetti. Amanda traveled from the US to study in Italy. Before traveling to Italy for her studies, Amanda attended the University of Washington. She was an ambitious student and her education was very important to her. Amanda's ambitious nature was apparent right out of grade school. She had her heart set on Seattle Prep because she had heard it was the most academically challenging high school in Seattle. She took the test and, not only was she admitted to Seattle Prep, she was awarded a scholarship. She didn't take this opportunity for granted. She excelled in her studies. Amanda graduated from Seattle Preparatory High School in the spring of 2005. After graduating high school, she attended the University of Washington, working toward a degree in linguistics. In the spring of 2007, she was named to the University of Washington's dean's list.

Amanda worked several jobs to save the money needed to participate in the study-abroad program in Italy. She left Washington to spend her junior year studying abroad as part of a yearlong course at the University for Foreigners. This was not Amanda's first quest to take in all the world had to offer. During the summer after freshman year, she participated in a student exchange program, spending three weeks living with a family in Japan.

Amanda was very excited about the opportunity to study in Italy. She found a job working part time at a local bar and she met a boy named Raffaele Sollecito at a classical music concert in late October.

Raffaele came from an affluent family. Raffaele is the son of Francesco Sollecito, a urologist from Bari. Friends describe Raffaele as a kind and caring young man who is always ready to give you a hand. Italy was completely new to Amanda, so meeting Raffaele most likely would have been comforting. Amanda and Raffaele hit it off from the start.

The future was looking bright for Meredith and Amanda. Both students were very happy with their decision to study in Italy and both had quickly adapted to their new environment.

November 1, 2007
Amanda and Raffaele had been dating for a short time. Their love was new and they enjoyed time alone. As Raffaele would explain in his diary, Amanda was spending her nights at his apartment and returning home the following morning to shower and change clothes. The morning of November 1 was no different. Amanda headed back to the cottage while Raffaele remained in bed. Amanda didn't care for Raffaele's shower and also had not brought any of her personal items or clothing to Raffaele's apartment.

For Amanda, the cottage was perfect. It was not in the best of locations, but that didn't seem to bother her. Although the space was small, it was more than adequate for a college student in Perugia. Her apartment was located on the second floor of a converted farmhouse built on a hilltop. The floor plan consisted of four bedrooms, two bathrooms, a small kitchen and living room area, a laundry room, and a walk out terrace. Amanda had fallen in love with the place from the first day she saw it. As a personal touch, she hung a sign on her bedroom door that read "Smile - it's the second best thing you can do with your lips."

This day was a holiday in Italy and many people would be traveling for the weekend. Meredith and Amanda's roommates had plans to be away. Laura was traveling to a town near Rome and Filomena liked to spend weekends with her boyfriend. Four boys lived in the first floor apartment, and they were also away for the holiday weekend.

Amanda saw Filomena briefly when she returned home. Filomena asked Amanda to help her wrap a present before Filomena left with her boyfriend for the weekend. Amanda and Meredith were having a conversation in the kitchen when Raffaele came by around 2 pm. Raffaele made lunch while Amanda played songs on her guitar for him and Meredith. Meredith took a shower, put a load of laundry in the washer, and left the cottage at around 4 pm. Meredith was going to spend the evening with friends while Amanda and Raffaele headed back to his apartment. Amanda was scheduled to work at Le Chic, a bar owned by Patrick Lumumba. She received a text from Patrick informing her that she was not needed at work. Little did she know at the time what a major impact on her life that text would have.

Raffaele learned that he was freed from his commitment to accompany his friend Jovana Popovic to pick up her suitcase from the bus station. Jovana stopped by Raffaele's apartment at around 8:40 that evening and left the message with Amanda. Not having to attend to their prior commitments left the couple the opportunity to have a quiet evening together and recover from the Halloween parties the previous day.

Amanda and Raffaele enjoyed a relaxing night together. As they would later explain, they prepared a meal, read a book, watched a movie, smoked marijuana, made love, and went to sleep. The only break in their evening came when Raffaele's sink leaked water all over the floor. Raffaele was a bit irritated because the sink had recently been repaired. Amanda calmed his mood when she said she would bring a mop from the cottage the following morning to clean up.

Meredith also enjoyed a relaxing evening with her friends. They watched a movie, ate pizza for dinner, and had apple crumble for dessert. Meredith's friends would later say that she was tired from the events of the previous day and decided to call it an early evening.

Meredith arrived home shortly before 9 pm. She
attempted to call her mother, but the call was interrupted.

November 2, 2007
Amanda left Raffaele's apartment around 10:30 am to
return home for her daily shower. When she arrived, she
found the front door of the cottage wide open. The open
door struck her as odd because everyone living in the
cottage always closed the door using the key. The door
was broken and the only way to keep it closed was to
lock it. Amanda entered the cottage and called out her
roommates' names but no one responded. At first she
thought that perhaps one of the girls had gone outside to
throw garbage away, or had run down to see one of the
boys below. She assumed someone had left, just for a
moment, leaving the door unlocked which caused it to
open.

Thinking about the possible reasons the door was
open, for the meantime, put Amanda's mind at ease and
she went to take her shower. When Amanda entered the
bathroom she noticed drops of blood, a spot of blood on
the mat outside the shower, and other stains in the sink.
She figured that the blood in the sink was from her ear
piercings a week prior that were still bothering her, while
other blood could be menstrual from one of her
roommates and they'd neglected to clean up.

After Amanda took her shower, she went to the other
bathroom to borrow a hair dryer and noticed someone
had forgotten to flush the toilet. Amanda had now seen

several oddities. The front door was open, there was blood in the bathroom, and there was an unflushed toilet. Amanda was concerned about the observations that she made. She grabbed the mop to clean up Raffaele's kitchen and returned to his apartment to discuss her concerns with him.

When Amanda arrived at Raffaele's, she tried to call Meredith and she also called Filomena. After Amanda told Raffaele what she had seen, they both decided to return to the cottage to take another look. Once there, they discovered that Filomena's window had been broken and they feared there had been a burglary. Meredith's bedroom door was closed and locked. They called out for anybody in the cottage and received no answer. Meredith had not mentioned any plans to be away for the weekend and Amanda was now growing even more concerned because Meredith was not answering her phone and did not respond when they called out her name. With the thought of a possible burglary, along with everything else they observed, they decided to try to open Meredith's door using force. Raffaele tried but was not successful. Amanda tried to see into Meredith's bedroom from the terrace. They also attempted to look through the keyhole on Meredith's door, but they still couldn't tell if she was in the room. Amanda went to see if the boys below were home and found they were gone. At this point Amanda and Raffaele decided to call Raffaele's sister who was a police officer. She urged them to call the Carabinieri (Italian Police). Amanda exchanged a series of phone calls with Filomena. Raffaele called the Carabinieri while Amanda made a call to her mother in Seattle to ask for advice. Shortly after Raffaele made the calls to the Carabinieri, two postal police officers arrived at the cottage.

The postal police were not responding to Raffaele's calls, but were investigating two cell phones that had been found in a nearby garden by an elderly Perugia resident, Elisabetta Lana. When the postal police arrived, they were greeted by Amanda and Raffaele, who were standing outside the cottage. The police had determined that one of the phones belonged to Filomena Romanelli, and they had come to the cottage to discuss the phones with Filomena to see how they could have ended up in the garden. As we know, Filomena wasn't home. The Carabinieri still had not arrived. As it turned out, they were having trouble finding the cottage. Amanda brought the postal police inside to show them what she had observed. In the meantime, Filomena was concerned about the situation at the cottage. After speaking with Amanda several times, she decided to come home. She called her boyfriend, Marco, and asked him to go to the cottage. The problem was, Filomena was out with her friend Paola and had left Marco without a car. Marco called his friend Luca, who happened to be Paola's boyfriend, and asked him for a ride. Within a short time the four arrived at the cottage. So let's recap. We have Amanda and Raffaele, two postal police, Filomena and

her boyfriend, and two other friends—all at the cottage—
and the Carabinieri still haven't arrived.

There was now strong concern for Meredith and the
decision was made to break down Meredith's door. The
postal police refused to damage property without just
cause so the job was left to someone else. Filomena's
friend Luca was the one to break the door down. A few
swift kicks did the job. Amanda and Raffaele were the
only ones that did not see into the room. Amanda was on
the phone with her mother and Raffaele was too far down
the hall to see. Filomena yelled, "A foot! A foot!"
Someone else shouted, "Blood!" Raffaele took Amanda
out of the cottage and the postal police took control of the
scene.

Everyone was ordered outside. The Carabinieri would
eventually show up in response to Raffaele's calls. They
would become part of a large group of people to quickly
assemble at the scene of this brutal murder. The cottage
rapidly became active with investigators. The press was
also quick to assemble. Photos were taken of the high-
profile officers as they arrived. Homicide Chief Monica
Napoleoni was one of the first on the scene. As time
passed, Perugia prosecutor Giuliano Mignini arrived
along with Edgardo Giobbi, the head of the forensic
squad in Rome.

Amanda and Raffaele watched everything from a
distance. Photos were taken showing them embracing.
Amanda was cold, and Raffaele would try to comfort her.
At one point, they shared a kiss. Amanda and Raffaele

didn't know it at the time, but at that moment, the world was closing in on them. Quick decisions were being made by investigators at the scene regarding the break-in, and members of the press were feverishly developing their opinions of the two based simply on a kiss.

Sleepless Nights

It would be the beginning of a series of sleepless nights as everyone present at the cottage was ordered to the police station for questioning. Amanda and Raffaele would catch a ride in Luca's car. Frank Sfarzo reported this drive to the station on his blog *Perugia Shock*. During the drive, Raffaele was discussing the details of the scene with Luca and Paola. Keep in mind, Raffaele and Amanda did not see into Meredith's room when the door was broken down, so Raffaele was looking for details. Raffaele asked if Meredith was dead and if she had been murdered. Luca responded that Meredith was dead and that her throat had been cut. All of this talk proved to be too much for Amanda. She broke down and began to cry. This conversation was to be of great importance because Amanda and Raffaele would later be accused of having had prior knowledge regarding the details of the crime scene. The conversation that occurred in Luca's car completely refutes that claim.

After arriving at the station, they waited as they were called in one by one for questioning. This time allowed those at the station to witness the emotions of the others. These observations would become very important at trial. Tensions would rise and exhaustion would set in as the questioning continued throughout the night; this would be the first of several sleepless nights for Amanda and Raffaele.

Meredith's British friends arrived at the station later in the day. Many were hearing of Meredith's death for the first time. Amanda and Raffaele had already known of the murder for a number of hours and had had time to gain their composure. They had also answered many questions at that point. Amanda described this time as exhausting. She stated that she was questioned for six hours straight and was only able to eat vending machine food that had given her stomach spasms. As Amanda would describe it, she had a "hell of stomach ache" until 5:30 in the morning. Meredith's friends at the station viewed Amanda's behavior as odd. They later commented that Amanda and Raffaele showed affection to each other while appearing cold and uncaring about Meredith's death. Amanda had learned about Meredith's murder five hours before Meredith's friends had arrived at the police station. Amanda was seen shaking and crying at the cottage when she first heard the news and she also broke down again in Luca's car. Meredith's friends were experiencing the emotions that Amanda had felt earlier in the day. Were these witnesses still unable to control their emotions five hours after they heard the news?

It's possible that Amanda's behavior did appear to be odd. She was in shock. Her friend was just brutally murdered. People experience many emotions during times of extreme trauma. There is no correct way to act and individuals often react differently. Amanda was seen crying and breaking down several times. If she was quiet and reserved at other times, she was simply dealing with the loss of her friend in her own way. You cannot decide guilt based on how someone reacts to a traumatic event.

The days leading up to the interrogation
From the moment Amanda and Raffaele arrived at the police station for questioning, they were being watched. Amanda stood out to investigators because her actions were foreign to them. Nothing she did was right. Every action was viewed in a negative light. Many of these details will be discussed later in the book. First, I want to lay out the basic details of the daily events leading up to the interrogation that took place on the evening of

November 5 through the morning of the November 6. The events of the days leading up to that night of the interrogation are very important because they clearly show that Amanda and Raffaele were sleep deprived and under extreme stress as that fateful day approached.

November 3, 2007
By this time, the media had flooded the area. Reporters from all over the world were now in Perugia. Amanda would spend the day being questioned by investigators. The police asked her many questions, as would be expected, but many pertained to Meredith's personal life. This was upsetting to Amanda, as she was not comfortable talking about Meredith's sex life. The line of questioning would only add more stress, as Amanda would later explain in her e-mail home. Amanda had not slept the night before and she had now faced another day of intense questioning.

That evening, Amanda and Raffaele went shopping to purchase underwear for Amanda. The cottage, of course, was a crime scene, and all of Amanda's possessions were unavailable to her. While in the store, cameras recorded the two as they shopped. At one point they were seen briefly smiling and sharing a kiss. Once again, an innocent kiss would be misrepresented in the press, providing more ammunition for those determined to assassinate Amanda Knox's character.

Shopping for underwear did not lead to what would later be insinuated in the tabloids. After Amanda paid for her purchase, the two had dinner and then met up with Laura and Filomena. Amanda described their conversation as a hurricane of emotions and stress. They discussed the shock that everyone was experiencing and were trying to figure out what to do for living arrangements.

Later that night at Raffaele's, Amanda could not sleep. She decided to send an e-mail home to update everyone on the events that occurred. Amanda sent the email to twenty five people on her e-mail list. I feel that Amanda was being very honest in her e-mail home and she was doing her best at a very stressful time to explain what had occurred up to that point. This e-mail would be scrutinized by many and far too much emphasis would be placed on the content. The e-mail showed nothing more than a young woman coping with a traumatic event by reaching out to those she knew and loved. You can see from the beginning of the e-mail that Amanda is expressing how stressful the situation was for her and it seemed that she just wanted to feel some comfort by communicating with people from home.

"This is an email for everyone, because I would like to get it all out and not have to repeat myself a hundred times like Ive been having to do at the police station. Some of you already know some things, some of you know nothing. What I'm about to say I can't say to journalists or newspapers, and I require that of anyone receiving this information as well. This is my

account of how I found my roommate murdered the morning of Friday, November 2nd."

Many of the details in the first two chapters of this book are based on Amanda's e-mail home. She details the events that took place leading up to the discovery of the murder and tries to give her friends and family a sense of what is happening. Accusations were made that Amanda was too descriptive with certain details. This was, in some way, supposed to show guilt. Many wondered why she put so much emphasis on the mop bucket or the unflushed toilet. The problem was that many would read this e-mail with a predetermined notion of guilt. With this approach, it may have looked as if Amanda was being overly descriptive with these particular details. In reality, Amanda was descriptive about everything. She wrote this e-mail during a sleepless night.

The e-mail rambled a bit and was very descriptive throughout. Here is an excerpt showing Amanda's detailed writing style:

"Another important piece of information: for those who don't know, I inhabit a house of two stories, of which my three roommates and I share the second story apartment. There are four Italian guys of our age between 22 and 26 who live below us. We are all quite good friends and we talk often. Giacomo is especially welcome because he plays guitar with me and Laura, one of my roommates, and is, or was

dating Meredith. The other three are Marco, Stefano, and Ricardo."

When Amanda described her living arrangements to those back home, she not only named each of the guys downstairs, but she gave their ages and discussed that one of them played the guitar. She was sitting at a computer typing whatever came to mind. These were not meticulously calculated words (as they would later be described), but rather a stream of consciousness.

The fact that Amanda mentioned the mop bucket was considered by some to be suspicious. Why did she feel the need to tell the people back home that she brought a mop to Raffaele's? She must have been intentionally pointing out the mop bucket as a reason to return to Raffaele's as part of some grand scheme, right? Well, this would certainly be the mindset of someone who viewed Amanda as guilty from the start. Yet it didn't look that way to anyone reading the e-mail, as they didn't have any predetermined notion. Amanda's e-mail was not complicated. She took a mop bucket to Raffaele's, so she mentioned it in the e-mail. There was no more meaning to it than that. Here is what Amanda wrote with regard to the mop bucket:

"I started feeling a little uncomfortable and so I grabbed the mop from our closet and left the house, closing and locking the door that no one had come back through while I was in the shower, and I returned to Raffaele's place. After we had used the

> *mop to clean up the kitchen I told Raffaele about what*
> *I had seen in the house over breakfast."*

Amanda was being crucified long before she ever had the chance to defend herself in court. Why were only some of the details in the e-mail questioned? Why wasn't Amanda questioned for mentioning that Giacomo played the guitar? She was writing home about a murder. Who cares that some guy living in the first floor apartment played guitar? Well, that detail doesn't make Amanda look guilty, so let's just ignore it. When you cherry pick only the details you like, you can create your own meaning with just about anything.

November 4, 2007
Amanda had now endured two sleepless nights and she found herself once again at the police station. She sat through another long session of questioning and that afternoon was told that she had to go to the cottage again to answer questions at the scene. Amanda was frightened to return to the cottage where her friend was murdered and this proved to be a very emotional visit for her. During the inspection of the cottage, Amanda was shown the knives in the kitchen and asked if any were missing. When she looked at the knives, she broke down and cried. All of her emotions flooded out of her at that moment. By that point in time, Amanda was suffering from extreme exhaustion.

After the inspection of the cottage, Amanda found herself back at the police station for yet another night. Raffaele had not been questioned since his initial statements on November 2, but he cared for Amanda and accompanied her whenever he could.

November 5, 2007

Amanda's education was very important to her. As everything seemed to be falling apart around her, she was determined to try and keep some control over her studies. She made the decision to attend class. The long holiday weekend had passed and it was now Monday. Amanda attended class and was able to complete the class assignment, which was to write a letter in Italian to whomever you chose. Amanda chose to address the letter for her assignment to her mother. This fact of Amanda attending class would later be attacked by the press. Amanda would also be vilified for the content of her letter. Amanda's mother was on her way to Italy and Amanda was looking forward to her arrival. Amanda would be criticized for discussing her own life and possible plans during her mother's stay, and not dedicating the letter to the memory of Meredith. This argument makes little sense seeing as the letter was written directly to her mother and not to the class. Of course her mother would not actually read the class assignment because it was written in Italian. The assignment was to write the letter as if you were writing to a specific person and that is exactly what Amanda did.

It was normal behavior for Amanda to describe her personal situation and to look for advice from her mother. This was a very uncertain time for Amanda. She was without a home, had no possessions, was being questioned relentlessly, and was grieving the loss of her friend. Amanda reached out to her mother for help and she was vilified for it.

Unfortunately, Amanda and her mother would not have the opportunity to spend any much-needed time together. That evening, Amanda and Raffaele would find themselves back at the police station for yet another night of questioning.

The All Night Interrogation

"All I know is that I didn't kill Meredith, and so I have nothing but lies to be afraid of"

Amanda Knox

Raffaele was the first to be questioned on the evening of November 5, 2007. The interrogators meant business on this night and no method would be overlooked to achieve the desired result.

The interrogation began around 10:15 pm; Raffaele was brought into a room for questioning while Amanda sat in a waiting room. Monitoring the interrogation was Edgardo Giobbi, head of the forensic squad in Rome. Soon after entering the interrogation room, Raffaele was told to remove his shoes and socks and hand over the contents in his pockets, which contained a pocket knife. They refused to give him back his shoes and also kept the pocket knife for evidence. They suspected that his pocket knife was used in the murder and they were hoping his shoes would be a match with the bloody shoeprints found in the murder room. It would not have been difficult for Raffaele to sense that he had become a murder suspect.

Raffaele asked to call his father, but the request was denied. Skilled interrogators attacked Raffaele vigorously with rapid-fire questions. They suggested to Raffaele that he couldn't possibly know what Amanda was doing when he was asleep. They repeatedly accused him of covering for a murderer. Raffaele did not hold up well against these well-seasoned interrogators. He became increasingly nervous.

Raffaele must have felt trapped in a situation that he had absolutely no control over. It must have been shocking for Raffaele to know he was now considered a suspect in a horrible murder. People he had been taught to have the utmost respect for were looking at him as a criminal for continuing to provide an alibi for Amanda, a girl he had only recently met. Raffaele knew he was not involved in any crime but was helpless to convince his accusers. Raffaele's sister was a police officer. Raffaele most likely had some understanding that anyone deemed a suspect could be locked up for as much as a year without being charged for a crime. Raffaele was in a desperate situation.

The interrogation was too much for Raffaele, and he crumbled. At about 11:20 pm, Raffaele signed a statement saying Amanda was not at his side for much of the evening, he didn't know for sure where she had gone, and that Amanda had asked him to lie about her whereabouts. Raffaele would later attempt to explain his statements in front of a judge, stating that he was under extreme stress; however, for this evening, the damage had been done.

Amanda Knox was interrogated through the night. Questioning was extremely aggressive. Amanda was in a situation in which she had absolutely no control. She was thousands of miles from home in a country where she had a very limited knowledge of the language. She was confronted by aggressive police officers who were accusing her of a horrible crime that she didn't commit. Amanda was terrified.

Amanda did not have a lawyer present during her interrogation. She was told it would be worse for her if she did. Amanda was told that she was being questioned as a witness, but she was clearly being interrogated as a suspect. Italian law is very clear; no suspect is to be interrogated without the presence of an attorney. The interrogation of Amanda Knox was illegal.

Interrogators are known to use several techniques to manipulate innocent suspects into self-incrimination. Over long periods of time, interrogators play mind games to confuse the suspect. One technique is to ask the suspect to imagine hypothetical scenarios. Interrogators feed information to the suspect for the suspect to imagine. During a long, drawn-out interrogation, the suspect gets confused and— in an attempt to comply with the request being made— begins to imagine the made-up scenarios. This is exactly what was done to Amanda Knox.

Physical force was also used on Amanda, and she was intentionally told lies leading her to believe the police had evidence against her.

Amanda stated in court testimony that she was repeatedly slapped on the back of her head and called a stupid liar. The interrogator who slapped Amanda told her that she was trying to help her to remember. Amanda was also told that they had proof that she was at the crime scene at the time of the murder. This was a lie. She was told that she was going to prison for 30 years and she would never see her family again.

Amanda was told that her boss, Patrick Lumumba, was the man that attacked Meredith. She did not give Patrick's name to the police; his name was suggested to her. The police took a text message on Amanda's phone out of context. The text from Amanda to Patrick ("See you later") was taken literally by investigators. In the U.S., this phrase, in the context that it was written, simply means "goodbye." The police told Amanda the text meant that she planned on meeting Patrick on the night of the murder. The police also left out the second part of the message: "Good night." When you put the phrase together, it explains the meaning even more clearly. Amanda had no intention of meeting Patrick that night. She was simply saying goodbye to Patrick in the text.

The interrogators told Amanda to imagine she was at the cottage. She was told to imagine that Patrick committed the crime. None of it seemed possible to Amanda. She tried to explain to the police that none of what they were saying made any sense. She knew that she was not at the cottage at the time of the murder. She had repeatedly told the interrogators the truth and now they wanted her to imagine something completely different.

They kept telling her over and over again to imagine that she was there. When she still could not imagine what they were saying, she was slapped across the back of her head. Once again she was told to imagine that she was there. She still could not do it. She knew what they were telling her was simply not true. She was scared and confused. After many hours of interrogation, with nothing to eat or drink, exhaustion started kicking in. Amanda was trying to remember, she was trying to help— but what they were asking her to say just did not seem possible.

Then came another slap across the back of her head. You stupid liar! You were in the cottage! You will spend 30 years in prison! You are protecting a murderer! You will never see your family again!

This abuse went on for hours until Amanda was finally broken. She was desperate to end the questioning. She was extremely confused and she could not take any more abuse.

After a long and grueling interrogation, suffering from extreme exhaustion with no food or water, twenty-year-old college student Amanda Knox gave in to the interrogators demands by describing an imaginary dream or vision. In this vision, she was in the kitchen covering her ears to block out screams while the man she worked for, Patrick Lumumba, was in Meredith's bedroom.

This so-called confession was typed out by the police. The confession was not written by Amanda Knox. At least 12 members of the police force interrogated Amanda. Why was it necessary for 12 people to interrogate a twenty-year-old female college student? Why were so many members of the Italian police force available to assist in an all night interrogation? Retired FBI agent Steve Moore provided an excellent answer to this question:

> *"If you are going to have 12 detectives available all night for an interrogation, you need to let them know well in advance. You need to schedule them, to change their days off, etc. You have to pay them*

overtime. In the real world, 12 detectives all night is something that has to be signed off by higher-ups. What does this tell us? It tells us the interrogation was NOT a rapidly unfolding case where lives were at risk—they planned this interview well in advance, and INTENTIONALLY overnight."

The interrogation was planned. The investigators were aware that Amanda's mother had just arrived in Perugia. Amanda would soon have a lawyer. They needed to act quickly. Every resource was put into action to break Amanda Knox.

In Italy, it is normal police policy to record interrogations. Amanda's interrogation was not recorded. Why wasn't the interrogation recorded?

Within 24 hours after the discovery of the murder, police were recording every cell phone call made by Amanda and Raffaele. Giuliano Mignini stated that he recorded the statements made by Amanda's flat mates and other witnesses. After Amanda was arrested, her phone calls from prison were recorded. Italian law requires that recordings be made of interrogations once a suspect is detained. Amanda was a suspect when she signed the final statement on November 6, 2007. Amanda's interrogation should have been recorded as required by law. Authorities claim they made no recording of their interrogation of Amanda. Mignini claimed it was an oversight. They managed to record everything else, but when the most important recordable event took place, they forgot to record it. This is simply not credible. Of course the interrogation was recorded. These recordings were withheld because they show that Amanda told the truth. If the public saw what had been done to Amanda Knox that night, it would destroy their entire case. Unfortunately, these recordings have most likely been destroyed.

The Italian Supreme Court ruled that the interrogation of Amanda Knox was inadmissible in the trial. The court stated that the interrogation was illegal because Amanda did not have an attorney present. The civil trial was running at the same time as the murder trial so the same jury heard the results of the illegal interrogation read to them anyway. Amanda Knox was interrogated illegally. The information obtained during the interrogation should never have been heard by any jury in any court.

Later in the morning of November 6th, 2007, Amanda hand wrote a letter explaining the interrogation. Amanda wrote:

"In regards to this 'confession' that I made last night, I want to make it clear that I'm very doubtful of the verity of my statements because they were made under the pressures of stress, shock and extreme exhaustion."

Amanda was very confused and she was scared. This did not seem to matter to the police. Amanda's illegal interrogation gave them the information they wanted.

As soon as they got Amanda to tell them what they wanted to hear, they went out and arrested Patrick Lumumba with no further questions asked. As it turned out, Patrick was innocent.

Amanda's statements about Patrick were completely unreliable. Amanda tried to explain to the police that her statements were made during a time of stress, shock, and extreme exhaustion— and that she didn't believe them to be true. After all, she was only repeating what the interrogators told her to say. At the time, the police simply didn't care. They arrested Patrick anyway. The police are responsible for Patrick Lumumba's imprisonment, not Amanda Knox.

I have included the full text of Amanda's handwritten note. Keep in mind, the handwritten note was written when Amanda was still suffering from extreme exhaustion. She wrote this just hours after her interrogation ended. Some people have taken this note out of context and tried to say that it was a confession. Amanda in no way confesses to the murder in her note. In fact, the note ends with this text.

"If there are still parts that don't make sense, please ask me. I'm doing the best I can, just like you are. Please believe me at least in that, although I understand if you don't. All I know is that I didn't kill Meredith, and so I have nothing but lies to be afraid of."

Amanda's words don't sound like a confession to me. I have included her handwritten note in its entirety so you will be able to read her words and reach your own conclusion.

Transcript of Amanda Knox's handwritten statement to police on the evening of November 6, the day she was arrested:

"This is very strange, I know, but really what happened is as confusing to me as it is to everyone else. I have been told there is hard evidence saying that I was at the place of the murder of my friend when it happened. This, I want to confirm, is something that to me, if asked a few days ago, would be impossible.

I know that Raffaele has placed evidence against me, saying that I was not with him on the night of Meredith's murder, but let me tell you this. In my mind there are things I remember and things that are confused. My account of this story goes as follows, despite the evidence stacked against me:

On Thursday November first I saw Meredith the last time at my house when she left around 3 or 4 in the afternoon. Raffaele was with me at the time. We, Raffaele and I, stayed at my house for a little while longer and around 5 in the evening we left to watch the movie Amelie at his house. After the movie I received a message from Patrik, for whom I work at the pub "Le Chic". He told me in this message that it wasn't necessary for me to come into work for the evening because there was no one at my work.

Now I remember to have also replied with the message: "See you later. Have a good evening!" and this for me does not mean that I wanted to meet him immediately. In particular because I said: "Good evening!" What happened after I know does not match up with what Raffaele was saying, but this is what I remember. I told Raffaele that I didn't have to work and that I could remain at home for the evening. After that I believe we relaxed in his room together, perhaps I checked my email. Perhaps I read or studied or perhaps I made love to Raffaele. In fact, I think I did make love with him.

However, I admit that this period of time is rather strange because I am not quite sure. I smoked marijuana with him and I might even have fallen asleep. These things I am not sure about and I know they are important to the case and to help myself, but in reality, I don't think I did much. One thing I do remember is that I took a shower with Raffaele and this might explain how we passed the time. In truth, I do not remember exactly what day it was, but I do remember that we had a shower and we washed ourselves for a long time. He cleaned my ears, he dried and combed my hair.

One of the things I am sure that definitely happened the night on which Meredith was murdered was that Raffaele and I ate fairly late, I think around

11 in the evening, although I can't be sure because I didn't look at the clock. After dinner I noticed there was blood on Raffaele's hand, but I was under the impression that it was blood from the fish. After we ate Raffaele washed the dishes but the pipes under his sink broke and water flooded the floor. But because he didn't have a mop I said we could clean it up tomorrow because we (Meredith, Laura, Filomena and I) have a mop at home. I remember it was quite late because we were both very tired (though I can't say the time).

The next thing I remember was waking up the morning of Friday November 2nd around 10am and I took a plastic bag to take back my dirty clothes to go back to my house. It was then that I arrived home alone that I found the door to my house was wide open and this all began. In regards to this "confession" that I made last night, I want to make clear that I'm very doubtful of the verity of my statements because they were made under the pressures of stress, shock and extreme exhaustion. Not only was I told I would be arrested and put in jail for 30 years, but I was also hit in the head when I didn't remember a fact correctly. I understand that the police are under a lot of stress, so I understand the treatment I received.

However, it was under this pressure and after many hours of confusion that my mind came up with these answers. In my mind I saw Patrik in flashes of blurred images. I saw him near the basketball court. I saw him at my front door. I saw myself cowering in the kitchen with my hands over my ears because in my head I could hear Meredith screaming. But I've said this many times so as to make myself clear: these things seem unreal to me, like a dream, and I am unsure if they are real things that happened or are just dreams my head has made to try to answer the questions in my head and the questions I am being asked.

But the truth is, I am unsure about the truth and here's why:

1. The police have told me that they have hard evidence that places me at the house, my house, at the time of Meredith's murder. I don't know what proof they are talking about, but if this is true, it means I am very confused and my dreams must be real.

2. My boyfriend has claimed that I have said things that I know are not true. I KNOW I told him I didn't have to work that night. I remember that moment very clearly. I also NEVER asked him to lie for me. This is absolutely a lie. What I don't understand is why Raffaele, who has always been so caring and gentle with me, would lie about this. What does he have to hide? I don't think he killed Meredith, but I do think he is scared, like me. He walked into a situation that he has never had to be in, and perhaps he is trying to find a way out by disassociating himself with me.

Honestly, I understand because this is a very scary situation. I also know that the police don't believe things of me that I know I can explain, such as:

1. I know the police are confused as to why it took me so long to call someone after I found the door to my house open and blood in the bathroom. The truth is, I wasn't sure what to think, but I definitely didn't think the worst, that someone was murdered. I thought a lot of things, mainly that perhaps someone got hurt and left quickly to take care of it. I also thought that maybe one of my roommates was having menstral [sic] problems and hadn't cleaned up. Perhaps I was in shock, but at the time I didn't know what to think and that's the truth. That is why I talked to Raffaele about it in the morning, because I was worried and wanted advice.

2. I also know that the fact that I can't fully recall the events that I claim took place at Raffaele's home during the time that Meredith was murdered is incriminating. And I stand by my statements that I made last night about events that could have taken place in my home with Patrik, but I want to make very clear that these events seem more unreal to me that what I said before, that I stayed at Raffaele's house.

3. I'm very confused at this time. My head is full of contrasting ideas and I know I can be frustrating to work with for this reason. But I also want to tell the truth as best I can. Everything I have said in regards to my involvement in Meredith's death, even though it is contrasting, are the best truth that I have been able to think.

[illegible section]

I'm trying, I really am, because I'm scared for myself. I know I didn't kill Meredith. That's all I know for sure. In these flashbacks that I'm having, I see Patrik as the murderer, but the way the truth feels in my mind, there is no way for me to have known because I don't remember FOR SURE if I was at my house that night. The questions that need answering, at least for how I'm thinking are:

1. Why did Raffaele lie? (or for you) Did Raffaele lie?

2. Why did I think of Patrik?

3. Is the evidence proving my pressance [sic] at the time and place of the crime reliable? If so, what does this say about my memory? Is it reliable?

4. Is there any other evidence condemning Patrik or any other person?

3. Who is the REAL murder [sic]? This is particularly important because I don't feel I can be used as condemning testimone [sic] in this instance.

I have a clearer mind that I've had before, but I'm still missing parts, which I know is bad for me. But this is the truth and this is what I'm thinking at this time. Please don't yell at me because it only makes me more confused, which doesn't help anyone. I understand how serious this situation is, and as such, I want to give you this information as soon and as clearly as possible.

If there are still parts that don't make sense, please ask me. I'm doing the best I can, just like you are. Please believe me at least in that, although I understand if you don't. All I know is that I didn't kill Meredith, and so I have nothing but lies to be afraid of. "

(End of Amanda's note)

How could this possibly happen?

I want to discuss the subject of false confessions. I want to make it very clear from the start: Amanda Knox never confessed to any crime. During her illegal interrogation, Amanda was pressured into accusing another man of the murder of Meredith Kercher. She was also pressured into stating that she was in the cottage at the time of the murder. Even though she never confessed to the murder, the results of her illegal interrogation were the same.

Many people simply cannot understand how anyone could be pressured into making statements they knew were untrue. Amanda Knox is in prison today because she was pressured to do just that. In Amanda's case, she didn't even write out the so-called confession. She didn't even speak the words. Amanda Knox signed a letter typed out by her interrogators. After a long, aggressive interrogation from at least 12 members of the police force, having been repeatedly slapped on the back of her head and called a stupid liar, Amanda signed her name on the prepared document.

There are many reasons why people end up giving a false confession. In Amanda's case, her statements were coerced. Coerced confessions unfortunately are not uncommon. Fear tactics such as direct threats, intimidation, or actual physical abuse are used to coerce suspects into falsely admitting guilt to a crime or, in Amanda's case, implicating another person.

All of these fear tactics were incorporated into Amanda's interrogation. Direct threats were used when she was told she was going to prison for 30 years and she would never see her family again. Intimidation and physical abuse were used when she was repeatedly slapped on the back of her head and called a stupid liar.

Coerced false confessions often involve long interrogations lasting many hours. The suspect is forced to go without food and water. The suspect is kept awake for long periods of time and gets so worn down emotionally and physically that he or she is more likely to give false statements in an attempt to end the torture. During the confession, the police suggest information to the exhausted suspect, which the suspect incorporates into the confession.

Amanda's interrogation lasted for many hours. She was already suffering from extreme exhaustion when her final night of interrogation began. The information for the so-called confession wasn't only suggested to Amanda, the police were kind enough to type out the entire statement in their own words. Amanda simply needed to sign it. As soon as the pen met the paper and Amanda signed her name, her life changed forever. Amanda Knox was a twenty-year-old college student visiting a foreign country. She was under intense pressure from at least 12 members of the Italian police force. She never stood a chance against these tactics.

Steve Moore described the technique used on Amanda Knox in far greater detail in an article that he wrote for Injustice in Perugia. Steve has personal life experience in this field and his expertise is of great value in understanding how Amanda's interrogators were able to convince her to sign the written statement. This is what Steve had to say regarding a technique that was used on Amanda:

> *"They used a technique that I unfortunately became aware of while serving overseas in counter-terrorism. We used to call it "tag-teaming." I am aware of its use by intelligence/law enforcement officers of other countries. It takes dozens of operatives/officers to make it work. Two officers are assigned for approximately an hour at a time to the suspect. Their prime responsibility is simply to keep the person*

awake and agitated. They do this for only an hour, because it takes a lot out of the detectives. After an hour, a fresh pair of "interrogators" come in. Again, the questions they ask are secondary to their main task—keep the person awake and afraid. By tag-teaming every hour, the interrogators remain fresh, energetic, and on-task. The suspect, however, becomes increasingly exhausted, confused by different questions from dozens of different interrogators, and prays for the interrogation to end."

Steve finished his article with a very important point. The information of value didn't come from what the interrogators achieved during the interrogation, it is what they failed to achieve that counts. Steve wrote:

"What the inquisitors did not achieve, however, speaks volumes of Amanda's character and innocence. No matter how hard they tried, and how manipulative and coercive they were, Amanda repeatedly denied ANY involvement in the murder, and the police could develop no feelings of guilt in her. This is not sociopathy, this is innocence. Note that in her note, she expresses empathy for the officers who had just subjected her to this abomination. Never once did she question her own innocence. And never did she experience any sense of identification with the accusations of the police. Amanda Knox is an innocent college girl that was subjected to the most aggressive and heinous

interrogation techniques the police could utilize (yet not leave marks.)

She became confused, she empathized with her captors, she doubted herself in some ways, but in the end her strength of character and her unshakable knowledge of her innocence carried her through.

Case Closed

A rush to judgment that led to the arrest of three innocent people

Lead prosecutor Giuliano Mignini was quick to take complete control of this case. Mignini's mind went to work creating a vision of how this crime took place. He believed the crime started out as a sadistic sex game that turned into a brutal murder when Meredith refused to participate. His fantasy of a group sex game gone wrong was based on nothing more than his imagination. This was not the first time Mignini had had these visions. He already had a history of dreaming up satanic ritualistic murder fantasies. In Mignini's mind, the sadistic sex game he was referring to was instigated by a young woman. The woman would lead the attack, ordering two men to force the victim to submit to sex, pushing the victim to her knees, torturing and killing her with one or more knives. Mignini dreamt up this story, wrote the script, and then began casting his characters.

Using the information that he acquired from the illegal interrogation of Amanda Knox, Mignini quickly assembled his cast. Amanda was cast as the lead. Amanda's boss, Patrick Lumumba, was cast in a supporting role. Raffaele Sollecito was cast as the boyfriend who was controlled by Amanda and would obey her orders.

Now Mignini's cast was complete . . . but something was wrong: Patrick Lumumba had an airtight alibi. This was not surprising. After all, Mignini wasn't basing anything on evidence. He was simply looking to cast characters for his script. The only evidence he had was a text message on Amanda's phone. As discussed in the previous chapter, the text from Amanda to Patrick ("See you later") was taken literally by the investigators. In the U.S., this phrase, in the context that it was written, simply means goodbye. This phrase was either lost in translation or was intentionally twisted by the investigators to get the result they needed. It is also possible investigators were targeting Lumumba because of the African hair that was purportedly found at the scene. Lumumba, of course, was African.

Meanwhile, the police—unlike Mignini—were looking for actual evidence. Investigators found a handprint on the bed at the crime scene. The fingerprints pointed to an African male named Rudy Guede. Shortly after the murder, Guede had fled to Germany. He was stopped in Germany trying to board a train without a ticket and was immediately extradited back to Italy. Mignini's storyline fell apart. Further investigation showed all of the evidence at the crime scene pointed to Rudy Guede. His DNA was found on and inside Meredith's body. He also left his DNA on Meredith's purse. His DNA was also linked to feces left in the toilet. Though it was not known at the time, later discovery indicated that all of the shoeprints set in blood belonged to Rudy Guede.

The evidence was clear. There was no evidence at all to suggest that Meredith was killed during a satanic, ritualistic group sex game. Rudy Guede attacked and murdered Meredith Kercher—and he acted alone.

The actual facts didn't matter to Mignini. He had already reported his fantasy to the press. The police held a press conference stating that they had evidence that all three killed Meredith because she refused to participate in a sex game. They boasted that the case was solid. They were even bold enough to announce, "Case closed."

Lead investigator Edgardo Giobbi boasted:

"We were able to establish guilt by closely observing the suspects' psychological and behavioral reactions during the interrogations. We don't need to rely on other kinds of investigation as this method has enabled us to get to the guilty parties in a very quick time."

This decision of guilt was achieved before Giobbi had even heard of Rudy Guede. Giobbi also stated that his suspicions were raised just hours after the murder when he'd seen Amanda at the crime scene swiveling her hips as she put on a pair of shoe covers. Amanda was considered guilty by the lead investigator before a single piece of evidence was even collected.

Giobbi even put a photo of Amanda Knox on his wall of Italy's most notorious criminals. Mignini was already being investigated for abuse of office in relation to another case, so I have no doubt that he was desperate to protect his fragile reputation.

It would be too embarrassing to admit their mistake and doing so could threaten their careers. Their initial theory had already achieved so much notoriety that any backtracking at that point would leave them looking foolish in the eyes of the world. Besides embarrassment, there are other possible factors (related to Rudy Guede) that may have led the authorities to stick to Mignini's script. These factors will be discussed later in the book. No matter what the motivating factors may have been, Mignini's desired outcome was very clear.

Mignini kept his original script intact. His fantasy storyline only required one casting change. Mignini simply removed Patrick Lumumba and cast Rudy Guede in the second supporting role. He now had his revised trio. His cast was once again complete.

Mignini achieved his goal with no evidence to support his fantasy. Even if you are somehow able to look past the lack of evidence, the storyline is ridiculous. Amanda Knox barely knew Rudy Guede. She saw him come and go on a few occasions because he played basketball with the boys that lived below Amanda's flat. Amanda did place him on a police list of visitors to the downstairs flat, but couldn't even provide his name. Raffaele Sollecito didn't know Rudy at all. Raffaele had only been dating Amanda for six days. Was it really credible to suggest that these three people, who were virtual strangers, got together to commit a brutal sex-crazed murder? Could it even be possible that these two young men would take orders from Amanda, a young woman that they both hardly knew? Add to this fact that there is no evidence to back up this story, the logical answer is no.

Mignini's story would be laughable if it wasn't so tragic. We are not actually talking about characters in a script. Mignini's story was all just ridiculous fantasy, but the people involved are very real. Would there really be any way for Mignini to get away with this obvious abuse of power? A judge would certainly see this case clearly for what it was. How could there have been any possible way that a judge would buy Mignini's story?

To see how Mignini was able to pull this off, we need to go back to the original suspects: Amanda, Raffaele, and Patrick. A preliminary court hearing was held for the three on November 8, 2007, in the courtroom of Judge Claudia Matteini. An honest judge would have immediately seen through Mignini's fantasy, but as reported by Candace Dempsey, Judge Matteini just so happened to be good friends with Mignini, so it was no surprise that the preliminary hearing did not go well for the accused. This was an extremely important hearing because it would decide whether or not the suspects could be held in jail for a year while further investigation was conducted. I find this aspect of Italian law to be disturbing. The defense attorneys were meeting their clients for the first time at that hearing. There was absolutely no way to prepare any type of counter-argument. If the judge believes the prosecution, the suspects go to jail for a year—it's that simple.

It was at this hearing that Raffaele would explain why he made contradictory statements during his interrogation (as discussed in the previous chapter). Amanda's handwritten note and Raffaele's statement in court were attempts to retract statements made under intense interrogation. These statements had no effect on Matteini's opinion of the two.

Judge Matteini released her decision, based on the information she was provided at the preliminary hearing, just one day later. In her decision, Matteini followed Mignini's script closely. Her decision was severely flawed for many reasons. Most importantly, as we know, Patrick would soon be released and Matteini had not even heard of the actual killer, Rudy Guede.

The details that Matteini used to justify keeping three innocent people in prison are very disturbing. If you allow yourself to take it all in, it will leave you feeling sick. All of the key pieces of evidence that she references have been completely refuted. Matteini bought the sex game gone wrong fantasy created by Mignini, and she based her argument on that theory. She placed Raffaele at the crime scene based on a shoeprint set in Meredith's blood in the murder room. She stated that Amanda and Raffaele were surprised by the arrival of the postal police and were "caught" with a mop bucket that was used during a cleanup effort. I am amazed at the storytelling that is allowed by the judges. Matteini suggested that Patrick wanted to have sex with Meredith because she had previously turned him down. Raffaele wanted extreme experiences and Amanda would have sex with anyone. All of these accusations were based on nothing whatsoever. Just like Mignini, Matteini was given the freedom to write pure fantasy.

There were no shoeprints from Raffaele in the murder room. All of the prints in the murder room belonged to Rudy Guede. Amanda and Raffaele were not caught with an incriminating mop bucket. The mop bucket in question had nothing at all to do with a crime scene clean up. Amanda and Raffaele were not surprised at all by the arrival of the postal police. In fact, they were expecting them. Raffaele called the police to investigate the break-in. Of course, as we all know, Patrick had an airtight alibi. This book will show in great detail how these accusations were completely discredited.

Judge Matteini was granted the power to make this very important decision before seeing any of the forensic evidence. In fact, she made this decision before Rudy Guede was even returned to Italy for questioning.

Not only did Matteini confirm the arrests, but she went even further to say that the suspects were a flight risk. This meant no chance at all of avoiding being locked up. Matteini would deny house arrest and was particularly brutal toward Amanda in her decision. Judge Claudia Matteini wrote:

"In such a situation the danger of repetition of the crime is certainly very high and can't be considered to have diminished due to the mere passage of time, during which -- as a reminder -- you have never shown any sign of remorse or reconsideration of your life."

It amazes me that this judge would expect to see remorse from Amanda Knox. This is just one more example of how guilt was decided from the start. It would be appropriate for the judge to state the evidence against a defendant. That is expected, of course, to show that there is enough evidence to hold a suspect. For her to suggest a lack of remorse demonstrates that this judge had decided Amanda's fate before she ever went to trial. Why would Amanda show remorse for a crime she didn't commit? Keep in mind—she hadn't even gone to trial to defend herself at that point. But this judge expected to see remorse.

I wonder if Judge Matteini would have come to a slightly different conclusion if she had waited for Rudy Guede to be returned to Italy. On November 20th, 2007, Rudy was arrested and Patrick was released. You would think this would cause a completely new investigation. But that was not the case. Rudy was simply inserted in Patrick's role in the script. There was never a single thought to look further into Judge Matteini's ruling. Amanda and Raffaele would remain locked up.

Amanda and Raffaele were given their chance to appeal the ruling made by Judge Matteini in front of the Supreme Court of Italy. Although a little progress was made at this trial when the court threw out Amanda's statement signed during her interrogation, for the most part the hearing was a complete failure. The court basically rubber-stamped Matteini's decision, buying into the sex game theory completely.

Rudy Guede's trial was set for September, 2008. Rudy chose a fast-track trial and was therefore tried separately from Amanda and Raffaele. Rudy was confronted with overwhelming evidence placing him at the crime scene. He admitted being at the scene but denied the murder. His story changed several times but none of his stories were credible. Guede was found guilty of murdering Meredith Kercher and was sentenced to 30 years in prison. His conviction was later confirmed on appeal but his sentence was reduced to 16 years. I will go into more detail about Rudy Guede in chapter eighteen. I will also discuss how a proper investigation could have discovered Rudy Guede as the murderer in the first 24 hours and could have avoided this colossal injustice. But that, of course, is just wishful thinking.

Many questions still remain on what actually fueled Mignini's actions that would begin this long, drawn-out nightmare for Amanda and Raffaele. Was Mignini writing a script merely to fulfill his vision of a sex game gone wrong, or were his actions something far more corrupt? Was he covering up an inexcusable error by the police? Was Rudy Guede a police informant? Did the police fail to prevent Meredith's death by not jailing Rudy when they had the chance? Why was Rudy miraculously let go every time he was brought into a police station? Who was authorizing his release? Amanda and Raffaele are entitled to hear the answers to these questions, but those answers may never come.

I highly doubt we will ever know exactly why the authorities acted as they did in this case; but one thing is clear, Amanda and Raffaele had absolutely nothing to do with the murder of Meredith Kercher. There is no justice being served by holding them in prison as this mess is sorted out. Amanda and Raffaele have already spent three years in prison for a crime they did not commit. During this lengthy period of time, not only have they fallen victim to a corrupt prosecutor, they have also been crucified by the media.

The Media

Media coverage of this case played a major role in the wrongful conviction of Amanda Knox and Raffaele Sollecito. Amanda was mistreated horribly by the media. The media took hold of this story and the disparaging headlines about Amanda were endless. These headlines were seen all around the world, long before any evidence was even collected. With the help of the media, prosecutor Giuliano Mignini's fictional character—the satanic, ritualistic sex-crazed killer Foxy Knoxy—was born. As we would all later find out, Foxy Knoxy was not a sex-crazed killer after all; she was a sweet, innocent eight-year-old soccer player. Amanda Knox was given the nickname as a child for her sly moves on the soccer field. By the time the world found out who the real Foxy Knoxy was, it was too late. The damage was done.

The media coverage was the strongest in the United States, the United Kingdom, and Italy. With Meredith Kercher being from South London and Amanda Knox from the United States, this was expected. Of course, Raffaele Sollecito is an Italian citizen, but the media was not overly concerned about him.

Amanda Knox became an obsession in Italy. Amanda Knox was named one of the top newsmakers of 2008 by countless Italian news organizations, alongside president-elect Barack Obama. It was not simply the fact that Amanda was receiving media attention; it was the amount of negative attention she received. The press declared Amanda Knox "a devil with an angel's face." She was called a she-devil: a diabolical person focused on sex, drugs, and alcohol. Her MySpace page was dissected. Photos that would normally be found on any twenty year old's MySpace account were perceived as sexual. A picture of her laughing while handling a machine-gun in a museum during a vacation with her sister was used to show Amanda as being a violent and unstable woman.

There was a series of lies leaked to the media shortly after Meredith's death. These lies were leaked for the sole purpose of destroying the credibility of Amanda Knox. Raffaele was almost totally ignored, leaving Amanda as the target of most of these leaks. The prosecution successfully used the media to assassinate Amanda's character. Amanda never stood a chance. She was found guilty in the court of public opinion long before her trial ever began.

Judge Francesco Cananzi, a representative of the national council of magistrates, said this publicly:

> *"Here in Italy trials take place on TV, rather than in court."*

Amanda Knox's lawyers have been outspoken about the abuse that Amanda received in the media. Carlo Dalla Vedova and Luciano Ghirga said Knox had come under "incredible and misleading" media scrutiny that they said was "in violation of the general principles that safeguard personal information and dignity. The media has done everything in its power to create an absolutely negative portrayal of Knox."

Amanda Knox had absolutely no history of violence in her past. She excelled in her studies and was named to the University of Washington's dean's list. Amanda worked several jobs as a student to save the money needed to participate in the study-abroad program in Italy. Why was the media so quick to turn against Amanda, long before any evidence was even collected?

Amanda was irresistible to the press. Her story had everything they wanted. She was a profitable headline.

Raffaele Sollecito was virtually ignored. Why? Because Raffaele was simply too boring to the press to be a profitable headline. The obsession with Amanda and the lack of attention given to Raffaele exposed the true intentions of the press. After all, Raffaele was being accused of the same crime, but every headline focused on Amanda Knox. Why? Because headlines depicting a beautiful, sex-crazed seductress committing murder during a drug-fueled orgy sold newspapers. Raffaele simply didn't have the same appeal.

Amanda Knox was vilified in the British press from the start. Some reports in the United Kingdom have been even more disparaging than the Italian press. One of Amanda's biggest enemies turned out to be the *Daily Mail*. Here are just a few of the ridiculous headlines from the *Daily Mail:*

"Foxy Knoxy: Behind the Hollywood smile, a liar, a narcissist, and a killer"

"Foxy Knoxy 'wanted to go shopping' after Meredith's murder"

"Foxy Knoxy claims female cell mate begs her for sex 'because I'm so pretty'"

"The Foxy Knoxy show: Smiling murder suspect makes grand entrance as trial begins"

This outright lie was printed after Amanda was wrongfully convicted:

> *"Amanda Knox: I got a fair trial... I appreciate American reaction but it doesn't help me"*

She said nothing of the sort. She said her legal team did a fantastic job. That was all she said. Amanda was obviously devastated by the ruling. You would never know this if you read only the *Daily Mail*. Of course, the *Daily Mail* offers tabloid journalism.

The more respected journalists in the United Kingdom must have been much more professional with the coverage, right? Think again. Even though the *Times London* had a more balanced approach, they still couldn't resist the salacious headlines. Here are some of the headlines printed by the *Times*:

> *"Amanda Knox: 'angel-faced killer with ice cold eyes'"*

> *"Amanda Knox tells of Meredith Kercher's 'yucky' death"*

> *"Amanda Knox, 'Foxy Knoxy', reveals her lesbian trauma"*

> *"Diary reveals Foxy Knoxy's sex secrets"*

They even printed this outright lie:

"Amanda Knox: I'm only a target because I'm sexy"

Amanda never made that statement. Amanda receives many letters of support in prison. She wrote about these letters in her diary:

"I think the same thing about this as I did before. If I were ugly would they be writing me wishing me encouragement? I don't think so. Oh, well, this is what my life is and I'll write to them and thank them for thinking of me." She adds, "Jeez, I'm not even that good-looking! People are acting like I'm the prettiest thing since Helen of Troy!"

Where does the statement *"I'm only a target because I'm sexy"* come from? This is an extremely twisted view of Amanda's actual statement. This is typical of the media when covering this case. The articles mentioned here are just a small sampling of the abuse that Amanda endured in the media.

Another disturbing observation regarding the media was the choice of photographs that accompanied their articles. When Amanda entered the courtroom, the cameras went haywire. Hundreds of photographs were taken of her over the course of the trial. Imagine if someone followed you around with a camera for one day.

Imagine how many different facial expressions you would make in the course of that day. Some of those expressions may only last a split second, but when a photo is taken, that split-second expression on your face is locked in time in that one photograph.

It was not only the written words that were designed to assassinate the character of Amanda Knox, the photographs that accompanied those words played a key role. Amanda would be vilified in the press for smiling as she entered the courtroom. Why would she smile in court? Amanda spends twenty three hours a day in a prison cell. When she entered the courtroom, she saw her family. She saw the people that loved her, and she smiled. This was a normal human emotion. Amanda smiled and the cameras flashed.

Barbie's Quest for Success

Careers are built on cases such as this. We often hear this in reference to members of law enforcement, but the same is true of journalists. Many journalists attempt to jump on stories like these to bring their names into the spotlight. I don't mean to paint a broad brush over the entire media. There have been several excellent journalists following this case. The unfortunate truth is many aspiring journalists tend to behave like bugs and hover around the brightest light. Barbie Latza Nadeau is one of those journalists. Barbie is a travel and dining columnist that writes for *Newsweek* and the Daily Beast. Barbie's articles center around Amanda Knox. She rarely talks about Raffaele Sollecito and almost completely ignores the murderer, Rudy Guede. It is very easy to see that Barbie has chosen to latch onto the one person in the case that can bring Barbie personal gain. When this approach is taken by a journalist, the actual facts often get pushed aside. Barbie has no interest in the facts; she only cares about furthering her career.

Barbie wrote an article that takes direct aim at the core of what the Injustice in Perugia website and this book stand for. Barbie's article titled "Friends Like These" discusses how the support coming from the United States is actually hurting Amanda and Raffaele. Barbie actually suggests that the support could "doom" Amanda Knox. Does Barbie realize what she is really suggesting? Does Barbie believe the court of appeals will actually use the support for Amanda Knox against her at trial? I would like to think they would base their decision on the actual evidence of the case. Barbie is insinuating that the Perugian justice system is a vindictive group that will exact revenge on Amanda for the words coming out of America. Does Barbie actually believe this to be true?

If Barbie's opinion is to be believed, then this belief would need to be applied to all trials in Perugia. This would certainly include the trial that resulted in the wrongful conviction of Amanda Knox and Raffaele Sollecito. This would mean that the ruling in the first trial must have been fueled by outside influences. I wonder if Barbie thought this out before printing it. Her article actually supports what many have felt for a long time:

that Amanda Knox was considered guilty in the court of public opinion long before her trial ever started. With Barbie's line of thinking, this would have certainly had an effect on the ruling by the court.

What if Barbie has another motivation for attacking the support that Amanda has received? What if Barbie herself feels threatened? How could this be possible? Well, it's simple really. Barbie's newfound success relies 100% on Amanda's guilt. Barbie is currently benefiting due to the suffering of others. If Amanda is exonerated on appeal, Barbie's career will take a hit. Barbie has written a book about this case and now has a possible movie deal in the works. Everything Barbie has going for her will all vanish if Amanda is freed. For this reason, Barbie should not be looked at as a credible journalist while reporting on this case. In fact, Barbie has no business writing articles about this case for *Newsweek*. I believe Newsweek has a responsibility to its readers to replace Barbie with an unbiased journalist that will report on the actual facts without any personal motivation. Barbie is a tabloid style writer. The Daily Beast is a perfect home for her.

In my opinion, Barbie is clearly being driven by money, and lost interest in the truth long ago. She proves this time and time again. In her article, she writes the following gem:

"The damage done by Knox supporters has, in some

ways, been almost worse for Amanda than the DNA evidence she left at the crime scene. "

This sounds good for the Daily Beast, but it is completely false. Amanda didn't leave any DNA at the cottage during the time of the murder. Amanda lived in the cottage! The DNA Barbie is referring to was not found in the room where the murder occurred—it was found in the bathroom that Amanda used every single day. There is absolutely nothing incriminating about Amanda's DNA in her own bathroom. There is no mistaking what Barbie is doing here. She knows the DNA is not incriminating. She doesn't care. Barbie's book and movie deal rely on Amanda's remaining in prison.

The above reference is not the first time that Barbie spread misinformation and outright lies regarding evidence at the cottage. Here is a quote from Barbie on MSNBC, April 10, 2010:

"There was a lot of information that was just never reported here in the United States...There were 5 spots of blood mixed... Amanda Knox's blood and Meredith Kercher the victim's blood found throughout the house in 5 different areas that were recovered after the use of luminol which is used to recover blood that's been cleaned up. "

First of all, Barbie loves to say that there was information not reported in the United States. Of course that's why we have the wrong opinion of the case. Barbie is well aware that the case has been covered extensively in the United States. There is no "secret" evidence that we are all unaware of. Besides, Barbie writes about the case for *Newsweek* in the United States. Maybe Barbie would like to explain why she decided to leave vital information out of her coverage.

Next, we look at Barbie's outright lies regarding the blood evidence. There were not 5 spots of mixed blood. Meredith's blood was collected in the bathroom Amanda and Meredith shared. The blood was deposited on surfaces that would have undoubtedly contained residual DNA from Amanda. This topic of mixed DNA will be discussed further in chapter ten. Barbie's statement that there was mixed blood in the bathroom is absolutely false. Even though it was not incriminating in any way, if Barbie wanted to report on the evidence collected in the bathroom, she should have reported that Meredith's blood was mixed with Amanda's DNA. Of course, telling the lie that it was mixed blood sounds much worse for Amanda.

Lastly, we look at Barbie's outright lies regarding the stains detected with luminol. Barbie is well aware that the stains detected with luminol were never proven to be blood. In fact, they were tested for blood and the tests were negative. Barbie also simplifies the explanation for luminol. From her explanation you would think that luminol only detects blood. The truth is luminol also reacts with many other things such as various household cleaners, different types of soil, rust in tap water, and many other substances. When luminol glows, investigators can pinpoint the area and then test to see if the stain does indeed consist of blood. The areas were tested for blood and the tests were negative. Does Barbie feel the need to discuss the actual facts of the stains detected with luminol? Apparently not.

I personally believe that Barbie is an excellent liar. She must be good because she continues to get away with statements she makes. I cannot say that Barbie's talent is one that I would be proud of, but I guess in Barbie's case, she just sticks with what she does best. She is also good at reporting the lies and misinformation of others that have long been refuted. In my opinion, knowingly repeating the lies of others as if they are facts is just as sleazy as creating the lie yourself. Barbie continues to spread the lie that Amanda was arrested for a disturbing the peace violation while living in Seattle. Here is an excerpt from her book:

> *"Her only brush with the law was a disturbing-the-peace arrest for a house party she threw."*

The truth is Amanda received a ticket for being a little too loud during a party she hosted. A photo of the ticket that was issued to Amanda has been available to the public for a long time now. In fact, this information was public knowledge long before Barbie wrote her book.

In a rare mention of Raffaele, Barbie continues to spread the lie that Raffaele purchased bleach to clean his apartment after the murder:

> *"When Raffaele was arrested, police searched his apartment and found a receipt for Ace brand bleach, purchased the morning of November 4, 2007, at 8:15."*

During a search of Raffaele's apartment, investigators collected all of the receipts in the house and held them up in from of the video camera. The video shows the receipt mentioned by Barbie. The receipt is not for bleach. Raffaele did not buy bleach to clean his apartment. Raffaele bought a pizza.

If Barbie would like to see the photo of the ticket issued to Amanda and the video capture of the receipt from November 4, 2007, I would be more than happy to provide them to her.

Barbie has shown her ability to write tabloid trash in her articles throughout the course of the trial. Her preference for tabloid journalism is also apparent in her book. The title *Angel Face* is depicted to be written in blood on the cover. It is quite obvious that the intention was to show the title written in Meredith's blood. This is a tacky cover, but not surprising coming from Barbie. I was most disgusted by Barbie's decision to describe Meredith's body in great detail. This served no purpose to the storyline and there was no need whatsoever to mention anything about the appearance of Meredith's private parts. Barbie chose to do this anyway. This clearly shows that Barbie will stop at nothing, no matter how immoral the action may be, in her quest for success.

Barbie has a very interesting take on how the murder took place. Here are a few excerpts from Angel Face:

"Between 9:15 and 11:15, Amanda, Raf, and Rudy got themselves seriously messed up; Amanda asked Meredith if she could lend her money to pay Rudy, and Meredith reluctantly did so."

"She prodded Rudy to go see Meredith; he went into her bedroom and started trying to kiss her and fondle her until she called out. Amanda and Raffaele went back to see what was going on, and instead of helping Meredith fend off Rudy, joined in the taunting."

"By this point, Amanda, Raf, and Rudy were beyond the control of conscience. Raf took a switchblade out of his pocket and started teasing Meredith with it. Rudy had a knife in his backpack and that came out as well. They had no intention of killing Meredith, but they were taunting her with knives on each side of her neck and she, in essence, impaled herself on the larger knife as she twisted in the grip of someone holding back her arms."

"The next morning, Amanda and Raffaele wake up around 6:00 A.M. with crippling hangovers and no memories of the night before. They peek into Meredith's room to find her battered and lifeless body, but they still can't remember anything."
"Rudy is nowhere to be found, and in fact, they don't remember that he was there. Amanda has a hazy recollection of a black man, but the only person she can think of is Patrick."

Barbie believes that Meredith impaled herself on the knife. According to Barbie, they were all just teasing Meredith and it was all just a big mistake. We are supposed to believe that Amanda and Raffaele committed a brutal murder and woke up the next day with absolutely no recollection of the act. Barbie's theory is ridiculous. Quite frankly, she should be embarrassed that this was the best she could do. Just like Mignini's theory, Barbie's is based on nothing but pure fantasy. I have little doubt why Barbie has chosen to attack those who support Amanda Knox. Barbie is only doing what she can to protect her own interests.

I would need to write another book to fully detail Barbie's deceitful reporting of this case, but I do feel the need to discuss one other article from Barbie titled "The Many Faces of Amanda." This article was printed in *Newsweek* in July, 2008.

Here is an excerpt from that article:

"And by her own account in a prison diary leaked to the media, she details her sexual escapades with at least seven men she'd been with in her three months in Italy before her arrest. She even wrote that she might have HIV and then she uses a process of elimination to narrow down who might have given it to her."

The truth is Amanda Knox did not have sex with seven men in Italy and her diary didn't say she had. In fact, corrupt prison officials had told Amanda that she might be HIV positive. Devastated by this news, as any person would be, Amanda made entries in her prison diary listing all the sexual partners in her life. These diary pages were taken from her and leaked to the European tabloid press, who reported falsely that Amanda's list referenced the sexual partners she had in Italy, rather than all of the partners she had in her entire life. *Newsweek* has an obligation to retract this lie furnished by Barbie Latza Nadeau. In the same article, Barbie goes on to misquote Amanda from her diary.

Barbie: *"I think it's possible that Raffaele went to Meredith's house, raped her, then killed her and then when he got home, while I was sleeping, he pressed my fingerprints on the knife."*

Here is the correct quote from Amanda's diary:

Amanda: *"So unless Raffaele decided to get up after I fell asleep, grabbed said knife, went over to my house, used it to kill Meredith, came home, cleaned the blood off, rubbed my fingerprints all over it, put it away, then tucked himself back into bed, and then pretended really well the next couple of days, well, I just highly doubt all of that."*

Here are some of Amanda's diary entries related to the lie that she might have been HIV positive:

"I had a raging headache because this is by far the worst experience of my life. I'm in prison for a crime I didn't commit, & I might have HIV."

"I don't want to die. I want to get married and have children. I want to create something good. I want to get old. I want my time. I want my life. Why why why? I can't believe this."

"Oh please please let it be a mistake. Please oh please let it not be true. I don't want to die."

It is very easy to see that Amanda was traumatized by the news that she might have HIV. In a very responsible manner, she put together an honest list of partners she had been with during her life. Little did she know that immoral journalists such as Barbie Latza Nadeau would use this information to formulate egregious lies to be used against her.

I have only cited a few of examples of Barbie's poor journalistic behavior. There are many more references that can be made throughout Barbie's articles and her book.

There is a journalist in the United Kingdom by the name of Nick Pisa that seems to follow many aspects of Barbie's journalistic playbook. It is no surprise that Barbie and Pisa are friends. Barbie had this to say about Pisa when acknowledging him in her book:

"to Nick Pisa, whose untouchable reporting skills and wit make him the true operatore"

According to a source in Italy, Pisa likes to hang around other reporters that are asking questions so that he can take notes. These are apparently the "untouchable reporting skills" that Barbie is referring to. Pisa is a freelance writer that seems to have differing opinions depending on whom he is writing for. This leads me to believe that he is void of any original thought. From reading his articles, it is my opinion that Pisa will write anything, without regard for accuracy, simply to cash a check. I cannot blame a guy for trying to earn a living, but much like Barbie, earning a living off of the suffering of others is detestable.

Here are a few headlines that accompany Pisa's articles:

"Compulsive Liar Foxy Knoxy Now insists she wasn't at House of Horrors"

"Lesbian Sex Plea to Knoxy"

"Foxy Knoxy plays the field from her jail cell with new romance"

"Revealed: Foxy Knoxy's sisters posing happily for 'macabre' photos at the house where Meredith died"

"Hayden banned from seeing sex monster Knox"

As you can see from the headlines above, Pisa does little to hide his intentions. When he is questioned about the headlines for his articles, he denies that he is the author. He claims that he writes the article and the paper provides the headline. I know this is often the case, but Pisa uses it as an excuse. He makes it sound as if he disagrees with the headlines but is powerless to stop them. In other words, his excuse is that of a weasel. If he had any credibility, he would not continue to write for a paper that tarnishes his work with sleazy headlines. Of course, all of this is just nonsense because Pisa's articles are often as deplorable as the headlines they accompany. Pisa should stop making excuses and admit that he loves the headlines because they bring him attention. Pisa is

71

nothing more than a tabloid hack earning a living off the suffering of others.

Unfortunately, Barbie Nadeau and Nick Pisa have not been the only embarrassments to journalistic integrity to follow this case in the media. Their behavior has been mimicked by many other aspiring journalists hoping to make their name off of this case.

Thankfully, not all media coverage of this case has been bad. Unfortunately, this coverage was playing in markets that had little effect on those that could make a difference. Most of the positive coverage has been viewed in the United States. Even though the programs are backed by factual information, being broadcast in the United States led many in foreign countries to write them off as biased.

CBS news stands out as an excellent source for factual information. The CBS Crimesider online series by Doug Longhini has been excellent. Doug is a no-nonsense writer that tells it like it is.

CBS *48 Hours* devoted an hour to Amanda, showing that she is the victim of a flawed investigation in a show titled "American Girl, Italian Nightmare." Paul Ciolino is a private investigator that was retained by CBS for this investigation. Paul has been attacked as being a biased reporter. The truth is Paul has excellent credentials. Paul is the lead investigative advisor to North University Law School's Center on Wrongful Convictions, the Medill School of Journalism, and DePaul University Center for

Justice in Capital Cases. He had this to say about this case:

> *"This is a lynching ... this is a lynching that is happening in modern day Europe right now and it's happening to an American girl who has no business being charged with anything."*

Paul hasn't been the only journalist to speak out about this injustice. Here is a small sampling of quotes made by other credible journalists.

Peter Van Sant: *"She's an innocent woman. And I would stake my reputation as a journalist [on that] and I have been in this business for a quarter century."*

Doug Preston: *"This is a case based on lies, superstition, and crazy conspiracy theories and that's it."*

Judy Bachrach: *"I have always thought that Amanda was going to go to a Kangaroo court and unfortunately I've been proven correct."*

John Q Kelly: *"This case is probably the most egregious international railroading of two innocent young people that I have ever seen... This is actually a public lynching based on rank speculation and vindictiveness. It's just a nightmare what these people are going through."*

Tim Egan: *"Preposterous, made-up sexual motives were ascribed to her...What century is this? Didn't Joan of Arc, the Inquisition and our own American Salem witch trials teach civilized nations a thing or two about contrived sexual hysteria with a devil twist?"*

I would like to personally thank Steve Shay for his advice and friendship as we both work to inform as many people as possible about this ongoing injustice. Steve has done an excellent job of reporting about this case for the *West Seattle Herald.* This is may be a small hometown paper, but with the far reach of the Internet, Steve's articles have been read worldwide. One of Steve's articles even garnered the attention of Giuliano Mignini, irritating him to the point that the *West Seattle Herald* was given the honor of being added to Mignini's growing list of lawsuits.

I applaud all of those who have stood up and spoken out about this injustice, but the sad truth is they have been no match for the negative press that has been spewing nonsense from day one.

As I predicted shortly after the conclusion of the first trial, we are now seeing a considerable shift in the media worldwide as the appeal trial gets underway. Many in the media that once vilified Amanda and Raffaele are now reporting that they may be innocent. I appreciate the fact that many have seen the error of their ways but it does not erase the damage they have caused. I am not ready to congratulate them for finding a higher moral ground.

Though some may have, others are just jockeying their position so they don't end up on the wrong side of the story.

I have lost a lot of respect for the media in recent years. I know the media is a business and I am certainly not naive to that fact. But I truly believe that the media has a responsibility to maintain a certain level of morality when lives are at stake. In this case, the lives of those involved were of no concern as articles in magazines and newspapers hit the newsstands and, more importantly, the Internet.

The Internet

This case has been a hot topic on the Internet, attracting worldwide attention. There is no denying that the Internet has played an integral role in shaping public opinion about this case. Pages of comments both for and against Amanda and Raffaele follow every article pertaining to the case. Many of these articles contain factual errors and some even contain outright lies. In the past, articles written for newspapers and magazines were read and then they'd disappear. Even if an article was blatantly false, it would be read and thrown in the trash. Times have changed. Once an article is posted online, it lives there forever. When you type Amanda Knox into Google, an article written about the case just days after the murder will be right there on your screen along with recent articles, as if it were just written today. The problem is the old outdated articles contain many errors. Some of these errors may have been the fault of the writer, but in many cases the information was not available at the time. Many details of this case that were written early on have long been refuted, but they still turn up in current debate. Why? Because the old outdated articles are still online. Unfortunately, many readers don't put as much weight on the date of the article as they do on its content. Many details mentioned in the media chapter quickly spread online.

The character assassination of Amanda Knox was fueled using information obtained on the Internet. Amanda's MySpace page gave the media her nickname "Foxy Knoxy." We are all now well aware of how that name was misinterpreted. Other information from her MySpace page was taken out of context and used against her. The photos on her account were among the first to begin circulating throughout the press. Many of the early leaks to the press spread very quickly. The prosecution's efforts to demonize Amanda were facilitated by the Internet.

It may seem like I am attacking modern technology and that I hold some sort of grudge against the Internet. This is far from the truth. I am simply pointing out how easy it is to abuse the power of the Internet to spread lies and misinformation. You can argue that the same technology is available to promote the truth as well. That is true of course, but early on, it was very difficult to compete with many news outlets that wanted to sell advertisements. Yes, I know it's hard to believe, but the media is driven by money. This is no different online than it is on television or radio. Everything is driven by money. The hot story was student killer Amanda Knox. The truth was not all that important.

The online coverage early on was not all negative. One of the most accurate blogs early on was *Perugia Shock*. Frank Sfarzo attended every court hearing and reported what he saw on his blog. He was one of the few people reporting from Italy in support of Amanda and Raffaele. He was not a proclaimed supporter. He was reporting the facts of the case and the facts were telling him they were innocent.

Candace Dempsey was another voice of reason online. Her blog *Woman at the Table* became a hotspot for debate. Candace reported from Italy as well as the United States, and she attended many of the court hearings. She was constantly attacked for reporting the truth. As I mentioned in the preface, she has written an excellent book, *Murder in Italy,* that I highly recommend.

Even though these voices were doing everything in their power to get the truth out to the public, their message was mostly drowned out by the massive media frenzy over Amanda Knox.

Websites were quick to come online on both sides of the debate. Support sites included *Friends of Amanda, Science Spheres, The Ridiculous Case Against Amanda Knox and Raffaele Sollecito,* and *View-From-Wilmington.*

These support sites all provided excellent information and inspired me to learn more about this case. I could see that those who supported Amanda and Raffaele had a different tone. All were presenting the honest facts of the case with no tabloid spin. These were honest people fighting a powerful media storm of misinformation that was impossible to overcome. After researching extensively, I knew I needed to do whatever I could to bring light to this injustice. With the help and guidance of those already fighting this battle, Injustice in Perugia came online shortly after the verdict.

The online debate surrounding this case has been ridiculous. I honestly feel that some people have an obsession with debating complete strangers online. Unfortunately for some, winning the online debate has become so important that they have forgotten that actual people are being affected. This is not a game. These are real people we are talking about, and innocent lives are being destroyed. This doesn't seem to stop the most fanatical posters. They will continue pushing misinformation and outright lies simply to recruit one more person over to their side. When the debate began, many were misled by the lies that were fed to them from the media. When these lies were completely refuted, many would see the truth and come full circle in support of Amanda and Raffaele, while others would simply refuse to back down from their position.

A friend and valued contributor to Injustice in Perugia, Michael C. Becker, recognized a clear pattern among many of the people speaking out against Amanda and Raffaele online. In their eyes, Amanda and Raffaele were guilty—and no evidence, or lack thereof, could change their minds. After observing this behavior for some time, Michael coined the phrase "guilter."

What exactly does guilter mean?
A guilter is someone that believes in the guilt of Amanda Knox and Raffaele Sollecito regardless of any evidence that is presented proving otherwise. A guilter will continue to believe that Amanda and Raffaele are guilty long after they are acquitted. Guilters are people that bought into all of the lies that were leaked to the press from the beginning of the trial to the present. Guilters continue to spread these lies long after they have been completely refuted.

Some guilters simply refuse to admit they made a mistake. For almost three years, guilters have been posting savage lies about Amanda Knox and her family. If they were to face the truth now, they would also have to face the fact that their behavior has been deeply unfair. Guilters will lie at all costs to hold on to their precious reputation.

Guilters have used this case as a way to socialize. They have become a group of friends that gather online to convince each other that Amanda and Raffaele are guilty no matter what the evidence—or in this case, lack of evidence—indicates. They feed off of each other's lies, assuring themselves that they have been right all along.

The guilters have organized a campaign online to spread lies and misinformation anywhere they can. Every article online is contaminated with their comments. YouTube videos quickly fell victim to the guilters. Support groups on facebook often fall prey to their vile comments. One of the most notorious guilters is Harry Rag. You will find his comments spread all over the Internet like a cancer. Hiding behind a fictitious name while posting lies and misinformation for the purpose of harming others is the behavior of a coward.

In addition to the comments posted throughout the Internet, there is a pro-guilt website that was created to push nothing more than pure hatred toward Amanda Knox and Raffaele Sollecito. The site links to a discussion board with a disturbing, cult-like atmosphere. I have no problem at all with an individual or group creating a website to voice their opinion. However, creating a website based on lies and the complete distortion of the facts in an attempt to destroy others is disgusting.

What makes the pro-guilt website even more reprehensible is the fact that it wraps its collection of lies in the memory of Meredith Kercher. The site is presented to the public as a memorial of Meredith, but it does not take long to see that this is not the case.

I have not included names of those involved because many hide behind screen names. Harry Rag is an example of that. Those that do use their actual names will receive no personal attention from me. It is my belief that the creator of the pro-guilt site is more interested in spreading hatred than paying tribute to Meredith. The site's creator appears to me to be not only obsessed with Meredith Kercher, but also with pretty dead girls in general. Photos of Natalee Holloway, Elizabeth Mandala, Laci Peterson, and Sonia Marra are posted. When you first visit the site, something just doesn't feel right about it. After you read a few posts, you see that it is outright creepy. In my opinion, much like Barbie Nadeau, the site's creator has an obsession with sex. He had this to say about me when he felt the need to talk about my daughter:

> *"Hmmm. Someone now tells me that Bruce Fisher who runs some FOA website claims to have a daughter. I have never paid much interest in him, but one has to wonder why he is slobbering kinkily over Amanda Knox while at the same time undermining those public institutions that are the bedrock of the future of his daughter and, when she has them, her own kids."*

Even though many of the people that support Amanda Knox and Raffaele Sollecito are women, the guilters like to spread lies that the support comes primarily from middle aged men that are attracted to Amanda. This line of thinking is disgusting, but not surprising. It is clear to me that these people are simply reflecting on their own obsessions when they describe others.

Besides spreading hate about Amanda and Raffaele and obsessing over other young female murder victims, the pro-guilt site also goes to great lengths to attack Amanda Knox's family members. Contests are held on the discussion board to see who can come up with the most sarcastic tagline for photos of Amanda's family. One poster made a photo collage of Amanda's sister crying at different stages of the trial simply to mock her. They don't stop with the adults in the family either. Both of Amanda's youngest sisters have been targeted. Photos of the two have been posted on the board and members of the group have even gone as far as attempting to gain access to their facebook accounts. These are innocent children being targeted by a group that claims to be running a site dedicated to Meredith Kercher. I would like for this group to explain to me how attacking Amanda's family preserves the memory of Meredith.

I find the attacks on Amanda's family to be some of the most disturbing behavior of the guilters, but many others are on their radar. The group does not hesitate to attack anyone who disagrees with them. One member created a cloned facebook account for Steve Moore's daughter in an attempt to impersonate her online. They also sent letters to Steve's former employer in an attempt to interfere with a current legal matter. One poster stated that his goal was "to bring down Steve Moore." Really? Good luck with that.

For reasons I cannot explain (other than perhaps a deep-seated obsession), the guilters like to view facebook accounts of those who contribute to Injustice in Perugia, often posting screenshots of the accounts on their site.

These are not the actions of a group that came together to preserve the memory of a murder victim. These are the actions of vindictive people that have built up a hatred for others they don't even know. Please keep this in mind when reading anything posted online that directly attacks Amanda and Raffaele. Please consider the source.

I understand that I risk bringing the guilters the attention they desire by discussing their actions and I know some will question why I have chosen to bother with them at all. I came to the conclusion that I could not talk honestly about the influence of the Internet on this case without discussing everything that transpired.

At one time the guilters had actually gained some popularity because there was an impression that their intentions were good. Over time the real agenda of the group has been exposed and a majority of the people that joined their group early on no longer participate.

In my opinion, the guilters that remain are only in it for themselves. Time and time again, their actions suggest that they do not care at all about Meredith Kercher. Just as an example, on the three year anniversary of Meredith's death, the conversation on the guilter discussion board was not one of deep thought and compassion. Instead, the group bickered back and forth with one poster repeatedly shouting profanity. What was the argument that was so important that it made it impossible for the guilters to behave in a respectable manner? They disagreed on how to handle a reporter that mistakenly reported on flowers left on the cottage gate to mark the three year anniversary of Meredith's death. The reporter said the flowers were plastic when they were allegedly silk. Yes, these people chose to argue about plastic flowers instead of reflecting on the person they claim to be memorializing. I know this may seem like a petty example, but it is reflective of the general behavior exhibited on the site daily.

At a time when the guilters should have shown compassion, they failed as usual. Instead they behaved as they always do: like children on a playground. I feel sorry for those who visited their site for the first time on that day hoping to see an honest memorial for Meredith Kercher. It is time for the few guilters that are left to stop misrepresenting their position. They need to stop stating that they started their site to pay tribute to Meredith and come clean with the truth. If this case was investigated properly, Rudy Guede would have been convicted as the lone attacker. This case would not have received worldwide attention. The guilters most likely would never have heard of Meredith Kercher and they certainly would not have created a website in her honor. Common sense tells you that the pro-guilt site was created to spread hatred of Amanda and Raffaele. Nothing more, nothing less.

Of course, my request to the guilters will never be honored. To them, it is we that are somehow being disrespectful of Meredith. As I have said many times, I do not think it shows any disrespect to Meredith Kercher to search for the truth. In fact, I feel that finding the truth in regard to her murder is the ultimate sign of respect to Meredith.

I understand that some people believe Amanda Knox and Raffaele Sollecito are guilty. These people do not belong to any pro-guilt group. They simply have the personal opinion that they are guilty. We are all entitled to our opinion. People want to believe that justice is served. People want to believe in law enforcement and the court system. Communities feel a sense of safety when bad people are put away. People that have faith in the justice system will fully respect the decision of the court when Amanda and Raffaele are acquitted. The guilters will continue spreading hate long after Amanda and Raffaele are back at home with their families.

It is fairly easy to separate an intelligent person voicing his or her opinion from a guilter. Simply look at the content of their comments. If you read the same old repeated lies about mop buckets, bleach receipts, *Harry Potter* books, showers in blood soaked bathrooms, buying sexy underwear and doing cartwheels, then you know you are dealing with a guilter. When you talk to a guilter, you rarely hear any facts—just a lot of hate-filled noise.

Is Wikipedia a credible source?

One of the most disappointing developments online is the complete destruction of the Wikipedia page detailing this case. From my observation, this page is heavily influenced by the guilter crowd. Several of the moderators that control the Wikipedia article have repeatedly shown bias. The current article contains many factual errors that are justified by Wikipedia because they are reliably sourced. The "reliable sources" that are used just happen to be the articles of misinformation that flooded the Internet shortly after the trial. These articles were discussed in chapter five. It is completely ridiculous that these articles are still considered reliable sources. When Wikipedia was contacted with factual evidence to correct the inaccuracies of the article, they were simply not interested in responding.

There is only one page currently allowed by Wikipedia in regards to this case. The current page is called "Murder of Meredith Kercher." Of course, I have no objection to this page. The victim of the murder should be the focus of the initial crime; but we all know that this case has become much more complicated over the past three years. Problems arise with the current format because any attempt to discuss the controversy surrounding this case on the Meredith Kercher page is considered off topic and is not allowed. I have no problem with this policy if another page were available to discuss all of the details of this case. Even though this has been called "the trial of the century" and hundreds of articles have been written discussing the controversy, Wikipedia refuses to allow a separate page for Amanda Knox. There is absolutely no explanation for this decision. Amanda Knox will be one of the biggest stories of the decade, yet Wikipedia not only chooses to ignore this fact, they prohibit anyone from creating a page to detail the events. How can Wikipedia be called an encyclopedia when they pick and choose what events in history they will permit discussion of? Why is Wikipedia allowing censorship of this information? It is quite obvious that Wikipedia is very determined to stop the truth from being discussed. The only article that currently discusses this case has been locked. No edits of any kind are allowed. Wikipedia explains that the page is locked because there are too many disputed edits. They claim the lock does not mean they support the current content. This statement from Wikipedia is ridiculous. Of course they support the current content. This information is currently available on their site for all to read. If there was such great concern for accuracy, the page would be taken offline as the disputes were handled.

You may ask why I am showing concern for one website when there are many websites available to present information. I am concerned because Wikipedia constantly finds itself at the top of Google searches. I honestly do not know if this is based solely on popularity or if Wikipedia has an agreement with Google. No matter what led to their search engine success, one thing is clear: many people get their information from Wikipedia. In fact, Wikipedia gets more attention than all websites discussing this case combined. It is very unsettling that misinformation keeps being fed to the public regarding this case.

The Internet is an amazing resource with the power to move information worldwide at lightning speed. This technology has endless benefits but can also be extremely damaging when the information being delivered is incorrect. The damage is often irreparable.

We know how this case was portrayed to the public. We know the world was fed lies and misinformation on a regular basis through all forms of media. Was there any truth whatsoever to the accusations being made? Was there any hard evidence to back up the information heard in the press leading up to the trial?

7

The Prosecution's Case

On Nov. 6, 2007, during the now famous press
conference declaring case closed, Perugian Police Chief
Arturo De Felice was being directed from behind the
scenes by Giuliano Mignini. He staked his reputation
along with the reputation of his entire police force on an
illogical theory. Even though Mignini was not present
during the press conference, there was little doubt that the
words spoken by De Felice were penned by Mignini
himself. From that day forward, the prosecution's case
was built. Guilt was decided before any evidence was

collected. The investigation worked backwards to find evidence to support guilt. This is not merely my opinion, this is a fact. Amanda and Raffaele were considered guilty long before anyone heard the name Rudy Guede.

So how do you go about collecting evidence with the absolute belief that you already have the guilty persons in custody? You cherry pick the evidence that fits your theory and throw away anything that contradicts it. All actions of the accused are to be looked at in a negative light. If Amanda claims she was not sure what time she ate dinner, she must be lying. When a witness claims to have heard a scream in the night but neglected to look at a clock, she is being truthful. When Amanda has confusion about the order of her phone calls, she must be lying. When Filomena has the same confusion about her phone calls, it's an honest mistake. When you take an unbiased look, there is nothing incriminating about forgetting the exact time you made a phone call. Both Amanda and Filomena did absolutely nothing wrong, but when you are cherry picking the evidence that fits into your theory, you take only what you need; you hold on to Amanda's confusion and you disregard Filomena's. When you use these tactics, you can build a mountain of evidence against anyone. In the end, what you have is a mountain of misinformation. In the next several chapters, I will detail the evidence that was presented by the prosecution, and I will show in great detail how the prosecution's mountain of misinformation was created.

The first major flaw in the prosecution's case was the failure to establish a motive. You will hear generalized statements arguing that it is not necessary to establish a motive to secure a guilty verdict. In some cases, this is true. When you have a case based on circumstantial evidence without physical evidence linking suspects to a crime, then a motive becomes crucial. The prosecution made extraordinary accusations in this case—accusations that require extraordinary proof. This proof was never provided.

If a motive wasn't necessary or important to secure a conviction, you wouldn't have known it by the prosecution's desperate attempts to provide one. The prosecution presented at least five different motives for the murder before finally deciding that a motive simply wasn't necessary. I say *at least* five because Giuliano Mignini changed his mind so many times, I might have missed one or two of his suggested motives over the course of the trial. Here is a list of motives from Mignini:

1. Meredith Kercher was murdered because she refused to participate in a sex game. Raffaele read Manga comic books that had satanic themes. Raffaele's interest in this topic fueled a satanic sexual orgy. Meredith refused to participate in the orgy, so she was murdered. Amanda ordered Raffaele and Rudy to hold Meredith on her knees while Amanda stabbed her with a knife. There was never any evidence at all

to support this ridiculous claim. This was simply a fantasy dreamt up in Mignini's mind.

2. Drugs made Amanda Knox and Raffaele Sollecito crazy. They murdered Meredith in a drug-induced rage. Amanda and Raffaele admitted to smoking marijuana that evening, but no other drugs were reported. Marijuana is not a substance known to cause rage. All of the women living in the cottage smoked marijuana. This was hardly a solid motive.

3. Amanda and Raffaele murdered Meredith so they could steal her money. It was pointed out to Mignini that Amanda was an extremely hardworking young woman. Amanda worked three jobs to save up enough money so she could travel to Italy for her studies. Amanda had a job in Italy at the time of her arrest. She also had a family back home that was more than willing to provide financial support if she needed money. At the time of her arrest, Amanda had plenty of money in her personal account. Raffaele came from a wealthy family. The motive of theft was simply not realistic.

4. Meredith's murder was fueled by hate. Mignini claimed that Amanda hated Meredith, so she murdered her. The truth is Amanda and Meredith were friends. Text messages were shown in court displaying kind messages exchanged between

Amanda and Meredith. Shortly before the murder, Amanda and Meredith went to the chocolate festival together. Amanda and Meredith were together earlier on the day of Meredith's murder. Meredith, Amanda, and Raffaele spent time in the cottage together. Raffaele made lunch while Amanda played songs on her guitar for Raffaele and Meredith. Amanda said that she had many photographs of Meredith and herself on her personal computer. These photographs would have shown a growing friendship between the two women. The court never saw these photos because investigators damaged Amanda's computer beyond repair. No explanation was ever given for the damage.

5. Amanda was a natural-born killer—a naturally violent person. However, there wasn't one thing in Amanda's past to suggest this. Amanda had never shown anger to anyone. Amanda was an honor student with absolutely no violence in her past. This theory quickly evaporated.

During closing arguments, after all of his different theories had fallen apart, Mignini told the jury: *"There is no motive."* He was bold enough to say that the evidence was so solid that a motive simply was not necessary. From looking at all of his failed attempts, it is pretty obvious that a motive was important to him. His failure to come up with one forced him to take a different angle.

This should have been a major point of concern for the jury.

The reason Mignini was unable to come up with a credible motive for his multiple attacker theory is simple: Amanda and Raffaele have no history of violence or sexual aggression and have never been involved in any type of group sex act. There is no credible evidence that more than one person murdered Meredith Kercher, or that Amanda and Raffaele were present during the attack.

The court was no more successful than Mignini at finding a credible motive. The court claims the murder was fueled by smoking marijuana. There is no logic in this conclusion. Many people smoke marijuana in Perugia. Amanda and Raffaele were seen smoking only occasionally and usually in the company of others. They would occasionally smoke with Filomena and Laura or the boys who lived below. The boys downstairs had five marijuana plants growing in their apartment. One of the boys who lived below had even asked Meredith to water his plants while he was gone. Smoking marijuana does not cause rage.

Professor Taglialatela testified that marijuana use can lead to calmness and relaxation, with some loss of memory and impairment of reality. The testimony recounted studies of animals that experienced some memory problems after consuming marijuana. Taglialatela also stated the relaxing effect did not lead users to be aggressive or violent. Studies show that marijuana lowers tensions and thus does not promote criminal behavior during use.

Amanda testified that she smoked a joint after dinner on the evening of November 1, 2007. After she smoked, she was intimate with Raffaele, and then they both went to sleep. The court believes the joint Amanda smoked led to a desire to engage in erotic sexual violence. This logic contradicts expert testimony on the influence of this drug.

Friends of Raffaele testified that smoking marijuana had a calming effect on him. Their observations of Raffaele describe the behavior that you'd expect from someone who smoked marijuana. Smoking a joint did not cause Amanda or Raffaele to become enraged. There is no logical basis for this accusation.

Here are a few basic facts about marijuana. A 2009 study indicated that 74 million Europeans, or 22% of the total European population between 15 and 64 years old, indicate they have used marijuana. I certainly do not condone this behavior, but the fact is marijuana is a popular drug. I personally feel that smoking marijuana should be discouraged and fought with better education. My views are based on health and social issues. I do not, however, fear that marijuana will breed violent killers. There is no proof of any kind that smoking marijuana will turn you into a brutal murderer. Violent behavior such as murder has never been noted in any studies of marijuana use.

The court chose to ignore all the facts surrounding marijuana use when constructing its motive. The court concluded that the use of marijuana contributed to random aggression leading to Meredith's murder. This logic is simply not credible. Just like the prosecution, the court failed to come up with a motive for Amanda and Raffaele to have committed this crime.

It would be logical to think that the prosecution would need a very solid case based on physical evidence to overcome their inability to establish a motive. Unfortunately, as we saw time and time again, logic had little bearing on the mindset of the prosecution or the court.

The lack of motive should have been a red flag for Mignini long before the court ever attempted to establish one. If Mignini had followed the actual evidence in this case, the court would have never been burdened with attempting to establish a motive for Amanda and Raffaele, because they would have never gone to trial for murder.

The murder of Meredith Kercher brought great responsibility to Giuliano Mignini. Meredith's life was stolen from her. The prosecutor leading the investigation had a responsibility to see that justice was served. Nothing less would be acceptable.

Meredith was a spirited young woman living life and experiencing the world. I do not pretend to have known Meredith. From what I have read and from the pictures I've seen, Meredith was a beautiful young woman who was happy with who she was. She was enjoying life. She was a daughter that would make any parent proud. She deserved to have the opportunity to enjoy all that life had to offer.

Many people that are currently following this case never had the opportunity to meet Meredith Kercher. We have all learned from the words of her family and friends just how special Meredith was.

Meredith's story is one that keeps parents up at night. I cannot possibly imagine my daughter in Meredith's situation, and I cannot begin to imagine the pain that her parents live with on a daily basis. My heart goes out to the entire Kercher family.

No matter what conclusions you draw from this case, one thing is certain: Meredith's family, her friends, and the world lost a bright, beautiful young woman on the night of November 1, 2007.

Due to the gross negligence of the prosecution and the court, the person solely responsible for Meredith's murder will not receive the proper punishment for his crime. Rudy Guede has many years of freedom in his future. If he was properly put on trial as the sole attacker, he would have most likely received a maximum sentence in the first trial and would not have been shown leniency on appeal.

When the power of authority is abused, it has far-reaching consequences that affect many people. The prosecution and the court in this case failed on many levels. First, they failed to keep the citizens of Italy safe. Rudy Guede will still be a young man when he is once again walking the streets. We can only hope that Rudy has deep regret for his actions and that he won't kill again.

Next, the prosecution and the court failed to protect the rights of two innocent people by wrongfully convicting Amanda and Raffaele. This should give the citizens of Italy great pause. Any one of them could fall into the same trap as long as those involved in this case retain their positions of power.

Lastly, the prosecution and the court failed to bring justice for Meredith Kercher. This is absolutely inexcusable, and all involved must be held accountable.

As you read through the next series of chapters detailing the truth about the alleged physical evidence, you will be left to wonder how it was ever possible—no matter how corrupt the prosecution was—to secure guilty verdicts against Amanda and Raffaele.

Raffaele's Kitchen Knife

The knife was the prosecution's "smoking gun." The knife was reported throughout the world as "the double DNA knife." The prosecution claimed that Amanda's DNA was on the handle and Meredith's DNA was on the blade. That is pretty damning evidence. Well, it would be . . . if it were true. The truth is the knife was not the murder weapon at all. The prosecution never found the murder weapon.

Here are the facts about Raffaele's kitchen knife. The knife was a common kitchen knife retrieved from the kitchen of Raffaele Sollecito. The knife was chosen from the drawer because it looked clean. No other knives were taken from Raffaele's kitchen to be tested. One of the officers that testified at the trial said he used "police intuition" when choosing the knife from Raffaele's drawer. Officers testified that there was a strong smell of bleach in the apartment and that the knife looked exceptionally clean. Italian forensic police expert Patrizia Stefanoni testified that it had tiny scratches on the side compatible with intense scrubbing.

Take a look at your knives at home. Unless your utensils are fairly new, you will see small scratches, nicks, and blemishes all over your utensils. This is typical wear from normal use. Normal washing will leave small scratches on silverware and glassware. The knife in question had some scratches on the blade. This is hardly proof that it was subjected to intense scrubbing. Most likely the knife had been washed a few times— nothing more.

Officers testified that there was a strong smell of bleach in the apartment. Some insinuated that the apartment, as well as the knife, had been cleaned with bleach. No bleach was ever found on the knife. As far as the smell in the apartment, Raffaele's maid cleaned the apartment the previous day with Lysoform, which also has a very strong smell. Lysoform does not actually contain bleach. The police simply smelled a recently cleaned apartment.

No matter what opinions were formed regarding the collection of the knife, proper forensic testing would reveal whether or not the knife was involved in the murder. Unfortunately for Amanda and Raffaele, proper testing was never done. Italian forensic police expert Patrizia Stefanoni performed the DNA testing on the knife. When the knife was tested, Amanda's DNA was found on the handle. This was expected because Amanda often prepared meals at Raffaele's apartment and she used the knife for cooking. A sample was taken from the knife blade and was tested for blood. The result was negative. There was no blood on the knife. What was left of the sample from the blade was tested for DNA. The results were negative. There was no DNA on the blade. Dr. Stefanoni's initial testing showed that there was no blood anywhere on the knife. No blood on the blade and no blood on the handle.

According to the prosecution, Amanda's DNA on the handle showed that she used the knife in the murder. How would Meredith's blood be missing from the same handle if the knife was used to kill Meredith? Cleaning of the knife would remove Meredith's blood along with Amanda's DNA. This clearly shows that Amanda's DNA was deposited on the handle at a different time, most likely when she used the knife to prepare food in Raffaele's kitchen. The negative blood test proves that there was no possible way that Amanda's DNA on the handle had anything to do with the murder.

When it came to the procedures used in Dr. Stefanoni's lab, all guidelines for testing DNA were thrown out the window. The sample found on the blade of the knife was too small to be tested using conventional DNA tests. Dr. Stefanoni would use her own version of a very new process called low copy number (LCN) DNA testing to test the sample. Many researchers believe that more development is needed before this technique is widely accepted. Conventional testing has been perfected in many laboratories throughout the world and has been properly validated over time. LCN DNA simply does not have the same reliability as conventional testing.

Dr. Stefanoni had neither the proper equipment nor the proper laboratory to perform low copy number DNA profiling, but she did it anyway. There are only a few laboratories in the world equipped to perform this type of testing. Her own lab was not even certified to perform ordinary DNA profiling at the time the tests were done. Dr. Stefanoni performed tests that do not conform to any standard anywhere.

Even with the low copy number method, Dr. Stefanoni was still not getting the desired result. The tests kept coming back "too low." To achieve the results she needed, Dr. Stefanoni took even more drastic measures by overriding the machine's parameters. Dr. Stefanoni pushed the parameters far past the level of reliability, finally producing the desired results. Keep in mind, the testing was done in a lab using large amounts of Meredith's DNA. Meredith's DNA was present in the lab, so it was very important that proper procedures be followed to make sure that contamination did not occur. Machines are set to proper levels for a reason. Tests that are too sensitive will produce false positives that are not reliable. Control tests should also be done. Control tests are done on other objects to see if contamination occurred. With the standards used by Dr. Stefanoni, many items in the lab could have produced a positive result from Meredith. Dr. Stefanoni's pen could have shown a positive result. How about her gloves? When you override the settings on the machine in a lab where Meredith's blood is also present, you could manufacture any result you wanted on any object. How do you prove this did not occur? Proper control testing is needed. Was this testing done? No. Dr. Mark Waterbury summed up the lack of control testing perfectly:

"Perhaps even more important for the knife DNA, no control experiments were run to follow the handling of the item from the field through to the laboratory. That is, to see if other, random objects retrieved from the same drawer and handled in the same, unprofessional way might also appear to have DNA on them. It would be interesting to hear the prosecution spinning a sinister implication out of DNA found on a can opener. Perhaps one can use canned peas for satanic rituals. Would Meredith's

*DNA be found on a spoon from the same drawer?
How about Filomena's? Would the spoon then be cast
as the murder weapon, whether it matches any
wounds or not? All this is preposterous of course. But
think about it. We have no way of knowing what the
supposed knife DNA means, or where it came from,
because no comparison tests of any kind were
performed."*

Dr. Stefanoni testified her job was to show objective
proof by precise analysis, including use of scientific
evidence. Her own notes reflect the DNA on the knife
blade was showing a finding of "too low." The testing
done on the knife also showed it was not blood. Dr.
Stefanoni initially stated that there was a finding of "a
few hundred" picograms. Information regarding testing
was withheld from the defense. When data was later
provided in July of 2009, it showed that the finding was
actually fewer than 10 picograms. Dr. Stefanoni created
her own form of LCN DNA to achieve the desired result.
To produce her finding, she ran the test once. This test
destroyed the sample; no other testing can ever be done.

Dr. Stefanoni had to hand-set the machine to get
beyond the "too low" finding, pushing the machine to
levels that are not permissible. Dr. Stefanoni's results
show findings below peaks of 50 relative fluorescent
Units (RFU), which make them unreliable.

Why would Patrizia Stefanoni try so hard to get the
desired result for the prosecution? The answer to that

question is a simple one. She needed to deliver the expected results to her boss, Dr. Renato Biondo. Biondo was not only the head of the DNA Unit at Polizia Scientifica, Rome, he was also a consultant for the prosecution. Dr. Mark Waterbury details just how dangerous the actions of the authorities were with regard to the DNA testing in his article "Amanda Knox: Canary in the LCN DNA Mine":

> *"How would you like to live in a world in which any person can be convicted of any crime, anywhere, any time, on the basis of unassailable, "scientific" evidence? The evidence will be unassailable because there will be nothing left of it by the time the analysis is through. They will be able to swab an object at a crime scene, LCN DNA profile it, and present it in court with no risk of contradiction. It will be their word against yours, and they will have a bunch of apparent, "scientific proof" backing them up. This is a recipe for a police state."*

The court completely ignored the defense when they rightfully challenged Dr. Stefanoni's procedures. Defense expert Professor Adriano Tagliabracci stated that the results from Dr. Stefanoni were not usable in any way. Dr. Stefanoni's testing was completely unreliable. Professor Tagliabracci noted incomplete documentation in Dr. Stefanoni's work and pointed out Dr. Stefanoni's notes where she had handwritten "too low" multiple times. Professor Tagliabracci stated that the reading of "too low" always means that the test should not be used for analysis. There are no exceptions.

Information regarding Dr. Stefanoni's testing was withheld from the defense until July of 2009. When Dr. Stefanoni's improper procedures were fully exposed, the defense requested additional testing by new experts. On October 9, 2009, the court rejected the defense request for additional testing. The court ignored all expert opinion and chose to blindly accept the results presented by the prosecution. The court had a scientific obligation to state the reasons to reject further testing. The court neglected to provide any reason for the rejection.

To date, some of the data files and documents that could show how contamination occurred in Stefanoni's lab have never been given to the defense. Information that was turned over in July of 2009 revealed inconsistencies and inadequacies that significantly undermine the reliability and trustworthiness of the results. The court ruled there was no doubt with regard to the results obtained by Dr. Stefanoni. The court believed if the result was readable on the machine at *any setting,* the result must be reliable. The court accepted what Dr. Stefanoni considered the only requirements needed for reliability instead of what the international scientific community standards demand.

Unreliable forensic testing is not the only reason the knife is not a credible piece of evidence. Professor Carlo Torre testified for the defense that Raffaele's kitchen knife is not compatible with the wounds on the victim. Professor Torre is a renowned forensic consultant in Italy who has worked on a number of high-profile cases. According to Professor Torre, the length of the fatal wound is 8 cm. There is bruising at the entry point showing that the knife was pushed in all the way to the handle. The handle caused bruising at the point of entry. The blade on the kitchen knife measures 17.5 cm. The other 2 wounds are too small to be considered compatible with the kitchen knife. The width of the kitchen knife is over 3 cm. The width of the two wounds that were not fatal measured 1.4 cm and 1.5 cm. According to Professor Torre, Raffaele's kitchen knife is not the murder weapon. The prosecution had to change their original theory that the kitchen knife was the only weapon used in the murder when it was shown that the knife was incompatible with the wounds on the victim. There were also photographs of a bloody imprint of a knife left on the sheet on Meredith's bed. The kitchen knife was too large to match the bloody imprint. When faced with this challenge, the prosecution simply changed their theory and stated that two knives must have been used. They provided no additional evidence to support this claim.

In the motivation report, the court tried to explain the additional knife. The court suggested that the small wounds on Meredith were caused by one of Raffaele's pocket knives. There was absolutely no proof to suggest this. The court simply made it up. Raffaele's knives were tested and were shown to have nothing to do with the murder. The knives were completely free from genetic material from Meredith. The prosecution provided no evidence whatsoever to suggest that more than one knife was used. The court not only provides no evidence to support its own theory, it also further discredits the prosecution's theory. The court suggested that Raffaele's kitchen knife and pocket knife were used in the murder. Neither knife matches the imprint on the bed sheet, which would mean that the court must be implying that three knives were used. What knife does the court want us to believe made the imprint on the bed?

Professor Torre stated that he saw no evidence to suggest that more than one knife was used. The smaller knife that made the imprint on the bed had the correct sized blade that would be compatible with all of Meredith's wounds. The large kitchen knife taken from Raffaele's kitchen drawer had nothing to do with Meredith's murder. Meredith Kercher was murdered with one knife. The murder weapon was never found.

Unreliable forensic testing and the fact that the knife does not match the wounds on Meredith completely discredits this piece of evidence, but we still need to look at how illogical it was to even consider the knife in the first place. There is no logical scenario of how Raffaele's kitchen knife was brought from his apartment to the cottage to be used in the murder.

The court does not argue that Meredith's murder was premeditated; it is suggested that the murder occurred due to a surge in erotic violence. There was no proof that Amanda had any interest in harming Meredith or had any growing resentment against her. If she had, it would have been displayed before resorting to murder. There is no proof whatsoever that Amanda had any intention of hurting Meredith before she was killed. The court made it clear that a sudden reaction occurred that caused the attack, so any knife used would have been one that was easy to grab and readily available. There were plenty of knives available at the cottage. The kitchen was well stocked with utensils; so well stocked, in fact, that Amanda had left a brand new set of kitchen knives stored under her bed because they were not needed. The point being, there were plenty of knives in the cottage that would have been readily available to be used in a sudden attack. These knives were visually inspected at the cottage and were eliminated as possible murder weapons by investigators early on, with no additional testing of any kind. When analyzing crime scene photographs, I was surprised to see that at least two of the knives in the cottage were very similar to Raffaele's kitchen knife. Of course, we know that this sized blade was not compatible with the wounds. However, if the prosecution accepted that Raffaele's kitchen knife could have been the murder weapon, then why quickly eliminate other similar knives without any further testing?

Unlike all of the knives at the cottage that were almost completely ignored, the knife retrieved from Raffaele's kitchen would obviously not have been readily available. Based on the court's explanation of the attack, the accusation that Raffaele's kitchen knife was involved in the murder made no sense at all. Faced with this dilemma, the court needed to get creative and come up with some way for Raffaele's kitchen knife to make its way over to the cottage.

The court created a scenario that suited their needs but was void of all logic and supported by no evidence. In fact, they even created dialogue for Raffaele that was completely nonexistent. In the motivation, the court suggests that Raffaele instructed Amanda to carry the knife around in her bag for her own protection. How did the court know that Raffaele made this suggestion? This suggestion was never brought up at trial, never documented anywhere, and no witnesses at any time ever heard Raffaele say anything of the sort. The court simply made up this suggestion without even thinking about how ridiculous it is.

The knife retrieved from Raffaele's kitchen is very large. The knife is over 30 cm long with a blade 17 cm long and a sharp tip. Let's put this in perspective: the knife is over a foot long with a nearly 7-inch blade. If the kitchen knife was carried in Amanda's cloth bag it would have torn through the bag and could have even been harmful to Amanda. The knife would have most definitely damaged the books and papers kept inside the bag, but this was not the case. Amanda's bag and contents were examined and found to have no cuts, tears, or damage of any kind. The prosecution also suggested that Amanda carried this knife in her bag for five or six days, yet no evidence confirms the knife was ever in her bag to begin with, and the court provided no witnesses that ever saw Amanda with the knife. The court's claims regarding the transport of the knife are illogical and, quite frankly, ridiculous.

When the evidence is properly analyzed, it is very clear to see that Raffaele's kitchen knife had nothing to do with Meredith's murder. I am not sure what is more disturbing: the methods used to give this piece of evidence credibility or the fact that the court blindly accepted those methods.

The Bra Clasp

The bra clasp is one of the most suspect pieces of evidence in this case. The prosecution went out looking for additional evidence against Raffaele because other evidence had crumbled. It was originally thought that Raffaele left a shoeprint in the murder room set in Meredith's blood. When this print was shown as belonging to Rudy Guede, the prosecution was left with nothing to prove Raffaele's presence at the cottage during the murder. They needed evidence in a hurry, or they would have to release Raffaele.

So, in desperation, the investigators headed back to the cottage on December 18, 2007. This was 46 days after the discovery of the murder. The clasp was originally photographed November 3, 2007, during the initial collection of evidence 6 weeks prior, but the investigators neglected to collect it. How this could have possibly happened is beyond me. When the bra was collected they should have observed that part of the bra was missing. It was imperative that both pieces be collected on the same day. Steve Moore discussed this blatant act of incompetence in his article titled Evidence Collection. He wrote:

> *"This is important evidence. If it's in another room, it could indicate that the assault started elsewhere. It MUST be found. It would be on our 'to find' list, much like the 'black box' at a plane crash. I would instruct that nobody leave that day until the bra clasp is found, or that I could definitively state in court that it was not in that house that day."*

When the clasp was tested, Raffaele's DNA was found on the clasp along with the DNA of at least four other people. None of these DNA profiles were found on the bra. How were all of these DNA profiles present on the little clasp but not on the actual bra? If the two pieces of evidence had been collected on the same day, these questions would most likely not remain.

It is highly likely that the additional DNA profiles found only on the clasp were due to contamination. The cottage was completely trashed by investigators during previous visits. Meredith's mattress was moved to the living room and her wardrobe doors were put out in the hall and then later moved back into her bedroom. Clothing was thrown all over the place. Investigators made very little effort to maintain any type of organization. All of this rearranging would have certainly led to dust and other matter being moved around the cottage. Foot traffic alone would heavily compromise any evidence discovered on the floor after any period of time. (See chapter fourteen for greater detail about the foot traffic.) The clasp was photographed in several different places on the floor throughout the course of the investigation. Somehow it kept moving around (as observed in photographs) until it arrived at its final destination under a dirty rug. It is clear that there was ample time for dust to accumulate on the clasp. A 2009 University of Arizona study showed that 40% of household dust is organic, primarily consisting of shed human skin cells. It is no surprise that mysterious DNA profiles were found on the clasp after it was eventually collected. Keep in mind that this clasp also had cloth attached to it from the bra. This cloth would have been an excellent dust collector.

So does all of this really explain how Raffaele's DNA was found on the clasp? Even though there are other factors to take into consideration regarding the DNA that will be discussed shortly, the events leading up to the actual collection of the clasp certainly show how Raffaele's DNA could have been innocently deposited on the clasp. Raffaele had only been dating Amanda for about a week at the time of the murder, but Raffaele had frequented the cottage during that time. Finding his DNA in the cottage would be no surprise. Raffaele had also attempted to break down Meredith's door on the day the murder was discovered. There is no doubt that Raffaele would have deposited his DNA in that attempt. It is easy to see that the possibility of contamination leading up to December 18 was very high, and more risk of contamination was still to come. The clasp was susceptible yet again on the day it was collected.

At least six investigators were present in the cottage collecting evidence and taking photographs. The crime scene video shows the investigators ignoring proper evidence collection procedures. The most blatant violation committed by investigators was the fact that they never changed their gloves. Those gloves quickly become contaminated. The investigators handled many items in the cottage before the clasp was collected and undoubtedly touched door knobs, light switches, doors, and many other surfaces as well.

To avoid contamination of evidence that may contain DNA, the U.S. Department of Justice lists the following precautions:

1. Wear gloves. Change them often.

2. Use disposable instruments or clean them thoroughly before and after handling each sample.

3. Avoid touching the area where you believe DNA may exist.

4. Avoid talking, sneezing, and coughing over evidence.

5. Avoid touching your face, nose, and mouth when collecting and packaging evidence.

6. Air-dry evidence thoroughly before packaging.

7. Put evidence into new paper bags or envelopes, not into plastic bags. Do not use staples.

In the crime scene footage, investigators are never seen changing their gloves. When the clasp was collected, no disposable instruments were used. In fact, investigators passed the clasp around the room, taking turns looking at it. At one point, it was dropped on the floor. You can see one investigator actually massaging the metal hook on the clasp using the finger of a visibly dirty glove. Raffaele's DNA was found on that metal hook.

So let's take a look at some of the items that were handled before the clasp was collected. We are able to tell what order the evidence was actually collected by looking at the sequence of photographs taken that day. Using this data, Ron Hendry created a timeline leading up to the collection of the clasp. Ron Hendry is a retired forensic engineer with 28 years experience evaluating and reconstructing serious to fatal incidents based on the physical evidence. He has done extensive analysis for Injustice in Perugia.

Investigation Timeline
The investigators arrived at the cottage at 1:14pm.

1:50 Investigators begin setting up a camera in Meredith Kercher's room

1:51 Items on and under Meredith's bed are examined

1:53 Meredith's wardrobe doors are moved to door entrance in the hall

2:01 Videographer begins taking video

2:04 Five investigators are viewed in living room

2:04 Investigator enters cottage with green cap; six investigators are now in the cottage

2:22 Floor is examined where shoeprints were erased by DNA scrubber

2:44 Floor is examined where Meredith's head had lain

2:49 Meredith's bedroom door is examined

2:53 The hall closet is examined, including mop and various cleaning products

3:12 The refrigerator is examined

3:18 The mattress is examined as it sits on the couch in the living room

3:22 Samples are stored in forensic kit in the hall outside Amanda's door

3:26 DNA sample is collected from the wall in Meredith's room

3:33 Meredith's shoes are examined

3:50 Meredith's handbag is examined

3:52 The clasp is examined and collected as evidence

Looking at the timeline, we can observe the key items that were handled in the cottage on December 18 before the clasp was collected. Meredith's door is a likely source of contamination. Raffaele acknowledged that he attempted to break the door down to see if Meredith was inside before the postal police arrived. Both of Meredith's wardrobe doors that had been removed from her room were resting on the outside door frame of her bedroom door. These wardrobe doors were later brought back into Meredith's room. It is very likely that contact was made with Meredith's door frame due to the fact that six investigators were working in a very small area.

Other items that were handled before the clasp included the supply briefcase the investigators had set up in the crowded hallway, Meredith's shoes, and the refrigerator. The supply case would have been a hotspot for contamination. All samples were brought to this location. The case was set up next to Amanda's door. Raffaele was in Amanda's room on the day of the murder. He could have easily left his DNA on Amanda's door. The hallway was so crowded that inadvertent contact with surfaces was nearly guaranteed.

Investigators' gloves could quickly have become contaminated from contact with Meredith's shoes. Meredith walked around the cottage in those shoes, so it is safe to say that the shoes could have contained Raffaele's DNA. Raffaele was at the cottage earlier that same day.

The refrigerator in any home is a central location for all residents. The door handle of a refrigerator would be one area where you would expect to find abundant amounts of DNA. Raffaele used the kitchen to prepare lunch on the day of Meredith's murder, so his DNA was quite likely on the refrigerator. The refrigerator is photographed in an open position, so it can be assumed that one of the investigators grabbed the door handle of the refrigerator with a gloved hand—the same gloved hand that would later come in contact with the clasp as the investigators passed the clasp around the room.

This discussion would not be necessary if the investigators changed their gloves after examining each item. Unfortunately, that was not the case. Their negligence led to several opportunities for investigators to contaminate the bra clasp. They would have undoubtedly come into contact with items in other rooms and locations of the cottage. These locations could have contained DNA residue from Raffaele that was placed there at an earlier time, completely unrelated to the murder. The clasp was not only susceptible to contamination during the six weeks before it was discovered; it was also susceptible on the day it was finally collected.

More about the DNA
The prosecution claimed that there was an abundant amount of DNA belonging to Raffaele on the clasp. This information circulated throughout the media leading up to and also during the trial. However, this wasn't the case. Raffaele's DNA was mixed with other DNA on the clasp. Meredith's DNA was present along with four other unidentified people. Raffaele's DNA accounted for only 1/6 of the total sample. The court's motivation report never even acknowledges the fact that the DNA is a mixture. It is simply ignored. This is not acceptable. The fact that the DNA is a mixture is extremely important. Not only does the mystery DNA on the clasp show almost certain contamination, it also lowers the genetic material that is attributed to Raffaele to well under 200

picograms, the standard minimum to be used for normal DNA analysis. In order for the sample to be tested properly, LCN analysis would have been necessary. The prosecution's experts did not perform LCN testing on the bra clasp. The defense stated that proper testing showed that some strands did not match Raffaele's DNA. The fact is, if *any* strands are not a match then it cannot be Raffaele's DNA. The defense was able to do limited testing. Additional testing will further confirm their argument. This additional testing will be requested and should be granted on appeal.

The location where the DNA was found was also suspect. The prosecution stated that the DNA was found on the metal hook of the clasp. This is not where we would expect to find the DNA if Raffaele cut the clasp off the bra. The prosecution claimed that Raffaele grabbed the clasp and then made the cut. Raffaele's DNA should have been on the fabric portion on the clasp. If there was any DNA from Raffaele on that metal hook it was most likely deposited there by the investigators that mishandled the clasp at the crime scene. The crime scene videos clearly show that the metal hook is repeatedly touched using dirty gloves. The DNA was purportedly found on the little metal hook of the severed bra clasp. There was no DNA attributed to Raffaele found on the fabric. A person trying to undo a bra holds the material on either side and slides it. If doing it violently, they may give it a strong pull, deforming the hooks, but in no case does a person actually touch or press on the hooks themselves when trying to open or pull and cut a bra. This means that DNA should be found on the material near the hooks— not *on* the hooks.

As with other evidence collected in this case, no control testing of any kind was done. This type of testing would have been very easy. The clasp was retrieved from under a dirty rug. Testing other items from that area to see if any of those items had also picked up DNA dust from the floor would demonstrate whether there was anything incriminating about the bra clasp. Of course, these questions remain unanswered because control testing was never done.

So here we have a piece of evidence that was completely mishandled during collection and then—to top it all off—the DNA results on this mishandled piece of evidence were misrepresented in court.

Defense expert Professor Adriano Tagliabracci stated that the clasp should be considered scientifically useless. I agree with Professor Tagliabracci.

Footprints, Shoeprints, and Mixed DNA

During the trial, assistant prosecutor Manuela Comodi presented the court with the footprint evidence that was detected using luminol. As expected, her job was to defend the police work of police forensic biologist Patrizia Stefanoni. Stefanoni claimed that Amanda Knox and Raffaele Sollecito's bare footprints, made in blood, were found on the floor. Comodi had the job of convincing the court that Stefanoni's findings were correct.

When evidence collection was completed on December 18, investigators sprayed the floor with luminol. What is luminol? Luminol is an investigative tool that can help investigators find blood after it has been cleaned up. When applied, luminol glows for a few seconds when it reacts with blood. Luminol also reacts with many other substances, including various household cleaners, different types of soil, rust in tap water, etc. When luminol glows, investigators can pinpoint the area and then test to see if the stain does indeed consist of blood. Stefanoni testified that these stains were never tested for blood; however, in July 2009, Stefanoni's notes confirmed the stains were tested with tetramethylbenzidine, which is extremely sensitive for blood. All of the stains detected with luminol tested negative for blood. Patrizia Stefanoni and Manuela Comodi chose to ignore the test results during the trial. The jury never heard the results of these blood tests; instead, they were subjected to this flawed reasoning from Comodi:

> *"At the scene of the crime there is a footprint made in blood on the bathmat and Knox and Sollecito's footprints made in blood on the floor,"* Comodi said, *"and these were supposedly made at some different*

*time because they stepped in bleach or rust or fruit
juice? It's up to you to decide."*

You decide? It is laughable that the prosecutor would be
so callous about something so important. How about this,
Ms. Comodi—why not show proof that the footprints
were made in blood? The truth is the footprints weren't
proven to have been made in blood. In fact, the glowing
luminol stains were proven to *not* be blood at all. But, of
course, you chose to ignore those test results in court.

The footprints were also swabbed and tested for
DNA. None of them tested positive for Meredith's DNA.
With this information available to the prosecution, how
could they possibly proceed with their accusation that the
prints were made in Meredith's blood?

Did these footprints really have anything to do with
this murder? The truth is these prints are undated. They
could have been made at any time by any of the residents
at the cottage. It was established from testing that the
prints were not made in blood. This should have
immediately eliminated the prints as evidence. Instead,
the prosecution chose to completely ignore this fact.

We can see from the photographs that several of the
luminol stains appear to be bare footprints, but what
convinced the prosecution that they belonged to Amanda
or Raffaele? The prosecution's expert, Dr. Lorenzo
Rinaldi, director of the print identity department of the
Italian police, claimed to have measured these glowing
footprints based on the photographs. Keep in mind, he

only had photos to work with and these were glowing images. It would be completely impossible to get the measurements exactly right; but, as Raffaele's defense expert Professor FrancescoVinci would point out in court, Dr. Rinaldi wasn't even close. Professor Vinci had clearly shown where Dr. Rinaldi had gone wrong. The reason that Dr. Rinaldi's measurements were incorrect was that he'd obtained an incorrect measurement of the floor tile. He used that tile measurement to calculate the size of the prints on the tile. Incorrect measurement of the floor tile changed the perspective of the prints.

In order to give these prints any relevance at all, we have to ignore the fact that they were not made in blood and that they were measured improperly. Common sense would tell you that the prints provided no information of value, but that was not the case during this trial. This evidence was somehow deemed credible. I will do my best to explain how this so-called evidence was presented at trial.

I will begin with the bare footprint that was located just outside of Meredith's door, toes pointing toward the room. This print was attributed to Amanda. Could this be possible? Let's try and make it work.

Amanda steps in Meredith's blood in the bedroom. She leaves no footprints at all in Meredith's room. She hops on one foot to the door, keeping her foot that is covered in blood elevated. When she gets to Meredith's door, she turns around and hops backward out of the room onto the once elevated foot, leaving one single footprint made in blood on the floor. Was all of the blood from her foot transferred in that one print, or did she simply start hopping on the other foot again? Tough decision? Okay, let's come back to that one.

The next two footprints I will discuss were located in the hallway. These blobs were said to be two right feet. The prosecution claimed that one of the footprints belonged to Raffaele.

Okay, once again, let's try and make it work. Raffaele steps in Meredith's blood in her bedroom. He hops on his left foot into the hallway. He then puts down his right foot one time making one footprint. The same question that applied to Amanda would also apply to Raffaele. Was all of the blood from his foot transferred in that one print or did he simply start hopping on the other foot again? At least with Raffaele he could hop forward. He had it easier than the backwards-hopping Amanda.

Wait, what about that other footprint? You know, the other right footprint adjacent to Raffaele's. Whom does that footprint belong to? Where did it come from? The prosecution did not care. They decided to skip it all together. Oops, I said skip. I think I meant hop.

Let's take a break from the confusion above and look at all of the shoeprints found in the cottage that were actually set in Meredith's blood. No luminol was needed to find these shoeprints; they were clearly set in blood and this was confirmed by testing. Can you guess who *these* prints belong to? Yes, all of the shoeprints seen in visible blood belong to Rudy Guede. Every single one of the shoeprints set in blood match the tread pattern of Rudy's shoes. He openly admitted the shoes belonged to him. He threw the shoes away when he fled to Germany. The box for the shoes was found in his apartment.

Okay, let's try to make this work. Here we go again, right? Where did Rudy hop around? What foot did he hop on? Did he hop backward or forward? The truth is, Rudy didn't hop around at all. His shoeprint pattern is very clear. He left shoeprints in Meredith's room and he left more in the hall. Rudy's shoeprints can be seen leading right out the front door.

We are not only supposed to believe that Amanda and Raffaele hopped all over the place, we are supposed to believe that they were able to clean up the stains found with luminol. We were even told that some footprints must have been cleaned up well enough so the luminol could not find them. We are supposed to believe that Amanda and Raffaele were able to achieve this amazing clean up without disturbing any of Rudy's prints and leaving no trace of their clean-up effort.

The prosecution presented no evidence whatsoever that proved that any clean-up effort took place. Bloody shoeprints from Rudy Guede's shoes lead down the hall and right out the front door. How could Amanda and Raffaele clean the floor removing all of the evidence that pointed at them while leaving all of the evidence that pointed to Rudy? This type of clean-up effort would simply be impossible. The prosecution's theory is nonsense.

Rudy Guede murdered Meredith Kercher. He acted alone. It takes a lot of imagination to try and make the footprint patterns show that Amanda and Raffaele were in the cottage when Meredith was murdered. It takes no effort at all to show that Rudy Guede was present at the time of the murder.

Carlo Torre, a professor of legal medicine at the University of Turin and a leading forensic expert, testified for the defense that any mixed DNA evidence of Amanda outside of Meredith's room was completely normal because she lived there. A person exiting a shower that was cleaned with a bleach-based cleaner and then walking on the floor would produce the results that were detected. Three of the stains detected with luminol were barefoot prints found in Amanda's room. It would be completely normal for Amanda to walk around her room after taking a shower. These prints cannot even be attributed to Amanda, but if they could be, there'd be a very logical reason for their existence. These prints did test positive for Amanda's DNA, but of course this would be expected because Amanda lived there. You would expect to find her DNA all over her room. Any prints that were made on the floor would mix with residual DNA that was already there. There would be nothing incriminating even if the prints in Amanda's room were made by her—the fact that even that point cannot be proven shows just how unreliable and completely useless the luminol stains are.

There were two shapeless stains detected in Filomena's room. The finding of DNA from both Amanda and Meredith was found in one spot in Filomena's room mixed with other unidentified DNA. This spot was not in a bare footprint, just a shapeless stain.

One luminol stain in the hall showed mixed DNA of Amanda and Meredith. This finding was a shoeprint left by Rudy. We can easily conclude that Meredith's DNA came from her blood on Rudy's shoe. Amanda's DNA is only found in this one shoeprint— not in any of the others. This was not Amanda's blood, just her DNA. Finding Amanda's DNA in the hall is normal. She lived there. The print on the floor would mix with the residual DNA already present. Why didn't they find any DNA mixed with Laura or Filomena? The simple truth is that they didn't look for it.

On the day the body was discovered, many people walked through the cottage. Many more people walked through the cottage in the days that followed the murder. After the cottage was considered a crime scene, many others strolled through. Investigators did not change their shoe covers when they walked from room to room. Contamination will be further discussed in chapter fourteen. As stated by Professor Torre, Amanda's DNA would have been expected to be found in the locations where it was detected because Amanda lived there. This DNA would have been deposited long before the murder occurred. It is also likely that the DNA was moved from one location to another after the murder occurred by the foot traffic inside the cottage. For example, DNA could have been dragged from the bloody shoeprint in the hall into Filomena's room. The evidence collected on the floor was heavily compromised by the time it was collected six weeks after the murder.

What about the bare footprint on the bathmat?
One of the myths surrounding the evidence in this case is that Rudy Guede's foot is too big to have made the print on the bathmat, but that Raffaele's foot is the right size. This is simply not true.

In fact, Rudy's reference footprint is longer overall than Raffaele's, but the forefoot region is neither longer nor wider. This part of Rudy's foot is actually a little smaller than Raffaele's. Moreover, the reference prints for both Raffaele and Rudy are longer in the forefoot region than the print on the bathmat.

The myth about the size of Rudy's foot is largely the result of the report that Rinaldi presented in court. He showed a side-by-side comparison of the dimensions of the print on the mat versus the dimensions of Rudy's forefoot. This exhibit does a good job of creating the impression that Rudy's foot is far too big to have made the print on the mat, but only because Rinaldi made a serious error in his measurements.

Jim Lovering (www.friendsofamanda.org) provided excellent analysis of the footprint on the bathmat. His analysis clearly shows that the prosecution's expert had the measurements wrong. Rinaldi completely miscalculated the size of Rudy's foot. Rinaldi stated the width of Rudy's foot was 66.7 mm when, in reality, his foot was 55.2 mm. Rinaldi's entire presentation was useless because he started with the wrong measurement of Rudy's foot. The truth is Rudy's foot was not too big to make the print on the bathmat. Was this incorrect measurement an act of negligence on Rinaldi's part or an outright lie? How could this expert use the wrong measurement for the floor tile when analyzing the luminol stains and also make this egregious error when analyzing the stain left on the bathmat?

Raffeale's defense team clearly points out in their appeal that the print on the bathmat was measured incorrectly. Proper inspection of the bathmat shows that the tip of the second toe blended with the top of the big toe. Rinaldi measured the big toe including the top of the second toe. This error caused the width of the toe to measure 30 mm. Rinaldi did not observe that the second toe had blended in with the big toe on the bathmat. The nature of the absorbent carpet may have led to natural spreading of blood. This print was made in bloody water, not pure blood. This would have caused spreading of the liquid as it was absorbed into the rug. This error in measurement is crucial because the prosecution based the compatibility of Raffaele's foot on the width of his big toe.

Raffaele's big toe measured 30 mm and is therefore incompatible with the measured foot on the bathmat.

When measured correctly, the print on the bathmat measured 24.8 mm. It is impossible that Raffaele's foot made the print on the bathmat.

It is not certain how the footprint was made, but evidence suggests the killer cleaned up in the bathroom, and several blood-soaked towels were found at the crime scene. It is very likely that the killer laid a bloodied towel on the bathroom floor so that it covered or overlapped the mat. He removed his shoe to rinse the blood from it. While his shoe was off, he stepped on the towel, transferring an imprint to the bathmat.

The outline of the foot is incomplete. The heel extends off the edge of the mat, and parts appear to be missing in the upper right and lower left quadrants. Using the scenario described above, these missing elements can be explained as areas where the towel was dry or where the foot extended beyond the edge of the towel.

There are unanswered questions regarding the print on the bathmat. This is often the case with evidence found at a crime scene. Some questions will never be answered. From the evidence provided, one thing is certain: Raffaele did not leave that print on the bathmat.

What about Amanda's shoeprint in Meredith's bedroom?

There were eight shoeprints, set in Meredith's blood, found in Meredith's room during the investigation. Six of the shoeprints were agreed to belong to Rudy Guede. Two of the shoeprints found in Meredith's room have been disputed. Rinaldi believed that two of the prints belonged to Amanda and Raffaele. Vinci showed the court in great detail that those two prints actually belonged to Rudy Guede.

The prosecution originally stated that there was one shoeprint matching Raffaele Sollecito's shoes found on the tile floor. They also stated that one shoeprint of a woman's size 37 shoe was found on a pillowcase. The shoeprint said to be a woman's shoe was attributed to Amanda.

The truth is, all of the shoeprints in Meredith's room match Rudy's Nike Outbreak 2 shoes. There were no shoeprints or bare footprints found in Meredith's room that can be attributed to Amanda or Raffaele.

The shoeprint found on the floor that was originally attributed to Raffaele was disproven early on by observations made by Raffaele's own family. This observation was made by counting the tread rings on Raffaele's Air Force One shoes. The photo showing the print on the floor had six rings, and Raffaele's shoes had eleven. Of course, Rudy's Nike Outbreak 2 shoes had six rings. Why did Raffaele's family have to point this out? Why didn't the prosecution's expert see that the prints clearly did not match? Rudy would later admit that the print belonged to him. Keep in mind, the crumbling of this piece of evidence caused the mad scramble to find something incriminating on Raffaele, leading to the discovery of the bra clasp.

As it would turn out, the alleged women's size 37 shoe was actually a partial shoeprint from Rudy's Nike Outbreak 2 shoe. There were a total of five shoeprints found on the pillowcase. Rinaldi only found two shoeprints. Vinci identified all five by highlighting the fabric using a process called Crimescope. None of these shoeprints represent a woman's shoe size 37. Rinaldi found one partial shoeprint on the edge of the pillowcase. It was that shoeprint that was said to be a woman's shoe. The truth is there were three partial shoeprints and all three partial prints match the tread pattern on Rudy Guede's shoes. Once again, Lorenzo Rinaldi had failed to properly examine the evidence. Once again, Professor Vinci set the record straight. Vinci's presentation cannot be disputed. He shows in great detail that the prints are a perfect match for Rudy's shoes.

Why didn't the prosecution's expert use the most advanced means possible to investigate the evidence? Why didn't Rinaldi use Crimescope? How could Rinaldi be so negligent so often? Even Raffaele's family was able to correct his errors. Rinaldi's work on this case showed complete negligence. It should be shocking to all observers that his work was considered acceptable by the court. Maybe we can gain a better understanding regarding Rinaldi's negligence by looking at who Rinaldi looked to for advice while doing his analysis. Rinaldi stated that he used the Grid of Dr. L.M. Robbins in his footprint analysis. By doing so, he affiliated himself with a thoroughly discredited junk scientist. Here is what the Chicago Tribune wrote about Dr. Louise Robbins:

"By the time Robbins died in 1987, appeals courts had overturned many of the cases in which she had testified. And the American Academy of Forensic Sciences, in a rare rebuke of one of its members, concluded her courtroom work was not grounded in science."

What about the mixed blood?

Much like the luminol evidence, the accusations made regarding mixed blood show how completely innocent circumstances were twisted to look incriminating. Somehow we are all supposed to be shocked that Amanda's DNA was found in her own home. The truth is there was no mixed blood—only mixed DNA.

Investigators found the mixed DNA of Meredith and Amanda in a total of six samples among dozens that were taken. Three of these samples were from the bathroom that Amanda and Meredith shared. The other two housemates used a different bathroom. Mixed DNA was also found in a latent shoeprint in the hallway. A swab from Filomena's room revealed Meredith's DNA with what appears to be a very weak profile for Amanda.

All of the mixed DNA samples from the bathroom were visible bloodstains. Most likely they were composed of Meredith's blood mixed with an organic residue containing Amanda's DNA. No test was performed to determine if any of these samples contained the blood of both Meredith and Amanda, and there is no evidence that any of them did.

The other three mixed DNA samples were taken from latent stains revealed with luminol. As mentioned in the previous chapter, Patrizia Stefanoni claimed these stains were never tested for blood, but we now know that Stefanoni lied.

The court has concluded that these findings are incriminating. This is not surprising. If you need to confirm a conviction and you have no credible evidence to do so, you have to come up with something.

The truth is the mixed samples that were found are not incriminating in any way. The most plausible explanation is that the mixed DNA is simply a result of cohabitation. As an example for the sake of comparison, investigators used luminol in Raffaele's apartment and found a latent stain with the mixed DNA of him and Amanda. This stain was the result of nothing more than Amanda and Raffaele having spent time at his apartment.

Here is an example that you can relate to in your own home. If you cut your finger and your blood lands on a sink in a bathroom shared by another person in your house, you will get the exact same result. Your DNA will be mixed with the DNA from the other person that also used the bathroom. All it means is that two people have been sharing the same space.

In addition, crime scene video clearly shows that blood samples in the bathroom were not collected properly. The collection swabs were used like cleaning rags. Large surface areas were wiped with one single swab, and on several occasions multiple surfaces were wiped down using one swab. Investigators never changed gloves during this collection process, leading to an even higher risk of contamination. If the DNA samples collected were not already mixed upon contact with the same surface, they were certainly mixed once they were collected on the swabs. I talk more about contamination in chapter fourteen.

When you hear about bloody footprints and mixed blood it certainly sounds incriminating. As with the knife and the bra clasp, when you stop and look at the actual evidence regarding the alleged blood evidence, you see, once again, that the prosecution went to great lengths to misrepresent innocent circumstances in an attempt to make them appear incriminating. Did the prosecution put on a good show? Maybe. Was it the truth? Absolutely not.

Behavior

As we know, investigators determined guilt very quickly. In fact, the decision of guilt was made just a few days after the murder. Lead investigator Edgardo Giobbi determined the guilt of Amanda Knox and Raffaele Sollecito before he had even begun to collect or analyze any actual evidence. As mentioned in chapter four, the decision of guilt was reached before Edgardo Giobbi had even heard of Rudy Guede. These decisions were made by observing behavior rather than analyzing physical evidence. The behavior of Amanda and Raffaele was scrutinized on several occasions in a very short time frame. As soon as both were hastily considered guilty, their every action from that point would be viewed in the worst possible light.

One of the first accusations of suspicious behavior began with the arrival of the postal police. Raffaele was accused of suspicious behavior regarding his phone calls to the police. He was accused of running and hiding, making the calls after the postal police arrived. This would have certainly been suspicious behavior if it was actually true. Of course, this accusation was completely false. As discussed in chapter two, Amanda and Raffaele made the decision to call the police to investigate a possible break-in. Unfortunately for Raffaele, the lies that were put forth regarding the arrival of the postal police heavily influenced the decision to keep him detained until trial.

Here's what actually happened. The postal police were the first police to arrive at the cottage on November 2, 2007. They arrived to investigate two cell phones that were found in a nearby garden. The postal police handle this type of incident. The Carabinieri (Italian police) arrived much later than the postal police. The prosecution claimed that Amanda and Raffaele were surprised by the arrival of the postal police. Raffaele stated that he had already phoned his sister and the Carabinieri before the postal police arrived. Raffaele's sister was a police officer at the time. Amanda and Raffaele were not surprised at all. They assumed that the postal police were the

Carabinieri responding to Raffaele's calls. Raffaele was accused of hiding in Amanda's room and calling the Carabinieri after the postal police arrived. This was simply not the case.

The video taken from a camera located in the parking garage across the street from the cottage supports Raffaele's claim. The clock on the garage camera was ten to twelve minutes slow. The prosecution totally misled and confused the public on this point. The prosecution repeatedly stated the camera timer was fast. The prosecution was wrong.

The reason we know the clock is slow is because the camera shows a picture of a Carabinieri (Italian police) car and a Carabinieri officer with the distinctive stripe running down his trouser leg in a clip time-stamped 1:22 pm on the day Meredith's body was discovered. However, at 1:22 pm, the Carabinieri were driving around unable to find the place. They called Amanda's cell phone at 1:29 pm to ask for directions. Amanda handed the phone to Raffaele; he gave it to one of the postal police, who explained how to get there. That call lasted four minutes and fifty-seven seconds, meaning it did not end until 1:34 pm. Therefore, even if one assumes the call did not end until after the car appeared in the video, the clock had to have been at least ten to twelve minutes slow.

This is significant because it means the camera footage shows the postal police arriving after Raffaele called the emergency number. The claim that he went and hid in Amanda's room, called his sister, and then called the emergency number twice—a series of calls that took about five minutes—is nonsense.

Amanda's behavior would also come under attack when detailing the events that took place shortly after the postal police arrived. Amanda was accused of overreacting with regard to Meredith's door being locked. When you take an honest look at Amanda's actions, she really did nothing out of the ordinary given the circumstances. Amanda was worried about Meredith because of the observations she made in the cottage. The court suggests that there should have been no concern about the locked door because Amanda already stated that Meredith always locked her door. The court fails to realize that Amanda's concern was not only in regard to the locked door. She was concerned because of what she had observed in the cottage *in addition* to Meredith not responding to their having called her name and pounding on her door. This is completely normal behavior.

The court was suspicious of Amanda's behavior because she was more concerned than Filomena appeared to be at the time. Once again, this is an exaggeration. If you have a group of people, you will have different reactions to certain situations. Amanda was concerned by what she saw; Filomena had a different reaction, saying "Stupid Burglars"

Amanda explains her reason for concern during her interrogation with Prosecutor Mignini in December of 2007.

Amanda: Certainly. When the police came they asked, at least they asked Filomena, if that door was ever locked, and she said "No no no no, it's never, never locked." I said "No, that's not true that it's really never locked," because sometimes it actually was locked. But for me, it was strange that it was locked and she wasn't answering, so for me it was strange, but I wanted to explain that it wasn't impossible, that she did lock her door now and then.

Prosecutor Mignini: But usually, you remember her door being open.

Amanda: Yes it was usually open or at least...yes.

Prosecutor Mignini: But on that morning, understand that you were said to have stated that Meredith always locked her door. And that it was normal.

Amanda: I never said it was always locked. It's just that they didn't understand. I just wanted to explain that it was not always open.

It is clear to see that there was either a simple misunderstanding at the cottage between Amanda (who did not have a full grasp on the Italian language at the time) and the other native Italian speakers, or this was another case where an innocent event was exaggerated to make it appear incriminating. Either way, there was nothing suspicious about Amanda's concerns on that day. As it turned out, she had every right to be concerned.

Behavioral observations were once again noted as Amanda and Raffaele waited outside after the murder had been discovered. People see what they want to see based on predetermined notions. If you already have suspicions about a certain person, their actions may appear differently to you than to another observer who harbors no suspicion. Amanda and Raffaele were seen standing at a distance holding on to each other. At one point they shared a few small kisses. Photographs were taken and soon printed in newspapers and media outlets worldwide. The actual mood of the scene was lost in the photograph. All people saw was the kiss frozen in the frame. I mention the photos taken before and after this now famous kiss in the forward of this book. It was these images that led me to investigate this case further. My focus was on Amanda's facial expression. She looked terrified—as if something horrible had just occurred in her life. She was not embracing Raffaele in a sexual manner. She was looking for comfort in a time of extreme stress. When she shared a few light kisses with Raffaele, her facial expression of shock and sadness never changed. Amanda's expressions were genuine.

Something horrific had just occurred in her life; her friend had been murdered. The media should be ashamed of how they handled this moment. Anyone who looked at these photos without a predetermined notion of guilt would see absolutely nothing wrong with the behavior of Amanda and Raffaele in their time of sorrow.

Later in the same day, Amanda and Raffaele's behavior was observed in the police station. Meredith's English friends disapproved of Amanda's behavior. Amanda was very talkative and she was repeating herself often. They also disapproved of the affection between Amanda and Raffaele. At one point, one of the English girls wondered if Meredith had suffered. Amanda reportedly responded:

"What do you think? She fucking bled to death."

This statement was viewed as a cold-hearted response. I don't see it that way at all. To me this was a passionate response coming from someone who was very angry that her friend had just been murdered. I do not think Amanda's intention was to lash out at that particular person; she was just expressing her anger regarding the murder. As far as Amanda being talkative at the station, from what I have read, this was Amanda's personality. Add to that a high degree of stress. During times of extreme stress, people respond differently. Some may become very quiet while others are quite vocal. Neither behavior can be considered a sign of guilt. If Amanda and Raffaele had sat in the corner and not said a word, what would the response have been? Would they be considered guilty and afraid to talk? Nothing they could have done would have been correct. Every action can be spun and given a new meaning. The next chapter will go into more discussion regarding witness testimony. It would certainly seem that the testimony of Meredith's friends was influenced before they ever took the stand.

I know I am beginning to sound like a broken record when I say this, but when you have a predetermined notion of guilt you will view all actions of those presumed guilty in a negative light. This was very apparent when observing the reaction against Amanda simply for buying underwear. It was reported that Amanda went to a lingerie store with Raffaele shortly after Meredith's body was found to buy a G-string, and that both were laughing and talking about "wild sex" in the store.

This is simply not true. Amanda was locked out of her apartment because it was a crime scene. She needed underwear. As it turns out, the witness that said Amanda and Raffaele were talking about sex didn't speak any English at all. Amanda was speaking English in the store. It appears the witness was looking for his fifteen minutes of fame. Even though Amanda and Raffaele never discussed anything of the sort, poor translation from Italian to English and then back to Italian caused even more trouble in the press. Confusion between the words *hot* and *wild* led some people to believe that Amanda told Raffaele that she wanted to go home and have violent sex. The word *wild* is occasionally considered synonymous with the word *violent*. These things happen when witnesses tell lies to gain personal attention. The defense believes that a tabloid paid the witness for his story.

The sad truth is, the store wasn't even a lingerie shop. ABC's Elizabeth Vargas reported on the *Oprah Winfrey* show that she visited the store. She said they didn't even sell the sexy lingerie described in the media, and described the store as equivalent to a Target store in the United States. The security camera footage that shows a brief moment when Amanda smiled at Raffaele was all the media needed to spread this lie all over the world. This was one of the most widely distributed lies in this entire case. The media knows that sex sells. It doesn't matter whose lives get destroyed in the process.

On November 4, Amanda was brought back to the cottage to answer questions at the scene. As discussed in chapter two, Amanda was frightened to return to the cottage where her friend was murdered, and this proved to be a very emotional visit for her. During the inspection of the cottage, Amanda was shown the knives in the kitchen and asked if any were missing. When Amanda looked into the drawer, she broke down and cried. What authorities concluded from Amanda's behavior in this situation is a perfect example of how Amanda was viewed very early on: Amanda was accused of acting. The authorities believed that Amanda was faking her emotion to make it look as if she was distraught. Of course they would view her behavior in a negative light, because at the time they already believed she was guilty.

If you viewed her behavior without any predetermined notion, you'd see an entirely normal reaction to a very stressful time. This was the first time Amanda had been back to the cottage since the discovery of the murder. It would be reasonable to say that seeing those knives in the cottage, just a couple of rooms away from where her friend was murdered, could have caused the finality of the situation to hit home. We all go through a grieving period during times of loss. Reality sets in at different times for everyone. The grieving process is a personal one and we all deal with loss in our own way.

I believe Amanda was very distraught upon seeing the knives. Viewing the knife drawer forced Amanda, at that moment, to accept the reality that her friend had been murdered. Her outburst of emotion was a normal human reaction and shouldn't have been viewed otherwise.

Lifestyle choices and behavior were brought up regarding marijuana use as well as reading Manga comic books. These factors were said to have altered the behavior of Amanda and Raffaele.

The court suggested that smoking marijuana was a contributing factor that caused Amanda and Raffaele's participation in the attack of Meredith Kercher. This goes against what is known about the typical effects of marijuana use on behavior. Speaking for the defense, Professor Taglialatela, professor of pharmacology and toxicology at the University of Molise, had this to say regarding the common effects of marijuana use:

"the result is a state of relaxation and sedation, and then has a depressing psychological effect"

Gabriel Traverso, one of Raffaele's friends, testified that marijuana use had a very relaxing effect on Raffaele. Gabriel stated that Raffaele would become very calm and often fall asleep. Others offered the same observation. Scientific data clearly contradicts the allegations of the court about the effects of smoking marijuana.

If marijuana wasn't to blame then it must have been those evil comic books. This suggestion is ludicrous. The court believes that Raffaele was sexually aroused by comic books and wanted to experience extreme situations. The comics that Raffaele collected were Japanese comics, often referred to as Manga comics. Manga comics are imaginary stories that are very popular with people of all ages. Investigators collected these comics from Raffaele's apartment. The court completely misunderstood these comic books. Manga comics have a large following and enthusiasts organize fairs and theme parties revolving around the storylines. Manga comics are collected as a hobby just as many other comic books are. The hobby of collecting comics is as common today as it was in the past. Raffaele's Manga comic book collection has no relevance at all to this case and it is ridiculous to suggest that reading comic books would alter anyone's behavior to the point that they would be influenced to kill.

It is now clear how behavior was mischaracterized throughout this case. This continued throughout the course of the trial. As we know from the observations made in chapter five, everything Amanda did in court was scrutinized. It is mind boggling how people choose to view this case. This mentality continues to this day. A perfect example of this came when Amanda decided to have her hair cut short. The media went wild. What could this mean? What could have caused Amanda to take such drastic measures with her hair care? All of the questions regarding her haircut were ridiculous! Why on earth would anyone care more about Amanda's hair than her wrongful conviction?

I wish I were exaggerating about the reaction to Amanda's haircut, but I am not. After witnessing this mentality time and time again, it becomes very clear to see how simple it was to spread lies and misinformation about Amanda and Raffaele's behavior. After all, the lies that were told were much more exciting than the actual truth. Maybe we should be looking at the behavior of those covering this case as well as the behavior of those absorbing the information before we condemn Amanda Knox and Raffaele Sollecito for sharing a kiss.

Amanda Knox

Raffaele Sollecito

Above: The murder occurred in this cottage. The photo was taken in 2010 by Jim Lovering.

Below: Amanda's room showing the clothing she wore on the night of the murder; lying on her bed exactly as she described. This clothing was tested and nothing incriminating was found.

Above: An investigator taking a photo in the bathroom of the cottage.

Below: Investigators storing evidence samples at the cottage. They decided to set up shop in the hallway. The floor in this hallway would later be tested using luminol.

Above: Investigators trashed the cottage during their initial search. A dirty pair of gloves used during evidence collection can be seen discarded on the floor in the front room of the cottage. This is the same floor that would later be tested using luminol.

Below: The bra clasp is handled by multiple people wearing visibly contaminated gloves. Many more photos and videos can be viewed on the Injustice in Perugia website.

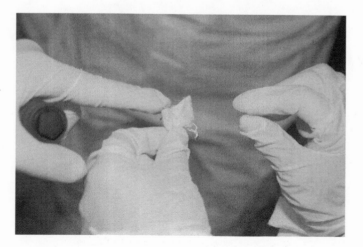

"Foxy Knoxy"

12

Staging

There has been much debate regarding the break-in that led to the attack and murder of Meredith Kercher. Very early on, authorities decided that the break-in was staged. This rush to judgment led to a very poor investigation. When you look at the window in Filomena's room, the evidence clearly shows that an actual break-in occurred.

It is honestly not surprising that the break-in was not more thoroughly investigated. As we know, evidence was being collected in an effort to support the presumed guilt of Amanda and Raffaele. An actual break-in would not only cast doubt on the prosecution's theory, it would completely discredit it. Simply put, if Rudy Guede gained entrance into the cottage through Filomena's window, based on theories put forth by the prosecution and the court, then Amanda and Raffaele are innocent.

As pointed out by forensic engineer Ron Hendry, the evidence available to investigators at the crime scene clearly showed a break-in. This crime should have been investigated as a break-in with intent to burglarize.

Unfortunately, investigators quickly concluded the break-in was staged, completely overlooking strong evidence suggesting an actual break-in took place. It was this mindset that led to the failure to properly investigate the window and Filomena's room. The question that still remains is whether or not the lack of investigation was by design.

Let's take a look at the evidence available to investigators at the scene. A rock was found inside Filomena's room. Evidence at the scene proved the rock was thrown from outside the cottage. The window has both inside and outside shutters. Both sets of shutters were unlatched. Filomena testified that she did not think she closed the outside shutters but she couldn't remember for sure. These shutters did not work properly and did not latch, so even if Filomena had pulled them closed an intruder would have been able to open them in seconds.

We know the rock came from outside because it damaged the interior shutter. There is a fresh mark on the wood of the interior shutter and small fragments of glass embedded in the wood. There is no other logical scenario for the broken window. The rock broke the glass and hit the inside shutter causing damage to the wood. As the rock made contact, it pushed open the unlatched shutter as it fell to the floor. As the rock traveled downward it caught the edge of a glossy black paper shopping bag that was sitting on the floor below the window. The rock knocked the bag over and came to rest on the tile floor on the edge of the bag. Crime scene photographs clearly show dust from the rock and small pieces of the rock that had broken free upon the impact of the rock hitting the tile floor. The impact of the rock caused glass fragments to fly across the room. There would have been no glass scattered in the room if the window had been broken from the inside to stage a break-in.

The prosecution stated that Amanda and Raffaele staged the break-in to frame Rudy Guede. The court was told that Amanda and Raffaele broke the window in Filomena's room and ransacked the room to make the murder look like a botched robbery attempt. Filomena went into her room several times on November 2, before the discovery of Meredith's body. She told the police that she saw glass from the broken window on top of her clothing.

The prosecution used her statement to make the case that the room was ransacked before the window was broken. There are many problems with this basic

assumption. A myriad of factors come into play. It is easy
to say, glass was on top of the clothes: case closed. But it
simply doesn't work that way. Did anyone stop to think
that perhaps the room was not tidy initially? I believe the
clothes were on the floor to begin with. I disagree with
the assumption that the room was intentionally ransacked
to make it look burglarized. I think the room was a mess
from the start. The clothes on the floor were not thrown
there to stage a break-in. The pile of dirty clothing was
already on the floor when Rudy broke the window.

Rudy broke the glass so he could release the latch and
open the window. After he entered the cottage, he most
likely searched the room for money. It would be
speculation to say what he was searching for. During his
search, it would be reasonable to say that he was moving
things around in the small room. The glass would have
been free to land anywhere. He would have most likely
left the room in disarray. There were a few items of
clothing that appeared to be lying folded on top of the
pile of unfolded clothes on the floor. Rudy may have
pulled a few items out of the wardrobe in his hasty
search.

Filomena was in her room several times the morning
after Meredith's murder looking for her belongings.
When she was searching her room, she likely would have
knocked some of the glass off the table or bed and onto
the floor—or anywhere else for that matter.

Investigators simply did not properly investigate the
room. They never checked to see if there was glass under

the clothes. There are no photographs showing glass on top of the clothes. There are two places on the floor where it appears that the clothes have been stepped on. There were no tests done on any of these areas. I believe there is dust on the clothes from the outside brick wall. I believe Rudy climbed up the wall, stepped into the room, and onto the clothes.

Ron Hendry did an extensive analysis of Filomena's window using high resolution photographs taken at the crime scene. Ron made a crucial discovery that was overlooked by investigators.

Ron discovered that shards of glass were physically pulled out of the wood window frame. Rudy most likely pulled the sharp pieces of glass out of the frame to avoid cutting himself as he reached in to unlatch the window. Photos clearly show that the frame was cleared of glass in several places. Glass on the ledge can be seen with clean edges that had been removed from the frame.

There is no way that Amanda and Raffaele would have thought to take this extra step if they had broken the window to stage the break-in. The removal of the glass from the frame shows definitively that the window was broken to gain entry to the cottage.

DNA test results from the cottage demonstrate that there was little investigation done inside Filomena's room. There were only five DNA samples taken from her room. In fact, they didn't even find Filomena's DNA in her own room, further proving that very little investigation was done regarding the break-in. Now we get to the second part of the prosecution's attempt to prove a staged break-in. The prosecution told the court that the window was too high off the ground for Guede to enter. The window was thirteen feet off the ground. That sounds pretty high, but the cottage provided a built-in ladder. The lower level windows on the cottage were protected with security bars. There just so happens to be a window directly below Filomena's window that could have easily been used as a ladder.

Rudy Guede is an extremely athletic young man. Just weeks before Meredith's death, Rudy broke into a law office. He entered the office through a window that was fifteen feet off the ground. He denied this of course, but Rudy was later caught in Milan with a computer and cell phone stolen from that law office.

The prosecution also argued that a nail on the wall below Filomena's window would have hindered Rudy's ability to gain entrance through the window. They argued that the nail would have been bent by anyone attempting to climb up to the window. This is simply not true. The nail could have been used as a temporary handhold as Rudy reached for the windowsill or the outer shutter. This action certainly wouldn't have bent the nail. Once Rudy was standing on the top row of bars of the lower window, his arms would have been at a higher level than the sill of Filomena's window. At that point, his arms would do the rest of the work. There would have been no need to use the nail as a stepping stone, nor would the nail have been an obstacle. There is no reason to assume the nail would have been used at all, let alone that it would have been bent. The nail argument was a very weak one.

The prosecution failed to prove that Rudy Guede would have been unable to gain entrance through the broken window. In fact, it would have been relatively easy for Guede. In October 2008, having sentenced Guede to 30 years in prison for the murder of Meredith Kercher, Judge Micheli said that climbing through that window would not require "a Spiderman."

We all know that Micheli is no fan of Amanda and Raffaele. Even he couldn't go along with the prosecution's incredibly weak attempt to show that the window was too high to gain entrance.

This is the one occasion where I honestly wish the prosecution was correct. If the window was too high or if the owner of the residence had installed security bars on that window as he did on the window on the first floor, Meredith might still be alive today. For the record, Filomena's window now has those security bars to protect the current occupants.

Staged crime scene

The prosecution claimed that Amanda and Raffaele returned to the cottage to stage the crime scene. This accusation by the prosecution relates to the staging of the murder itself. The prosecution stated that Meredith's body was moved to a different location and her bra was cut off by Amanda and Raffaele to make the crime look like it was committed by a lone attacker. Meredith was found covered with a duvet. The prosecution claimed that Amanda covered Meredith with the duvet because she didn't want to look at the corpse. Mignini boldly said that only a woman would cover the body. He insisted it had to be the act of a woman.

The prosecution stated that blood evidence proved Meredith was wearing her bra when she died. Mignini would describe this blood evidence in court:

"Nor is it just the blood on her bra which demonstrates this. It's also where the blood is not on her body. Meredith was wearing her bra normally when she lay in the position in which she died, and she was still wearing it for quite some time after she was dead."

This is simply not true. In fact, the photos of Meredith's body show small round droplets of blood on her bare breasts. She was on her back with her bra pushed above her breasts. She had an aspirating wound in her neck causing her blood to spray into the air and fall back down onto her body. The blood droplets landed on her bra and on her bare breasts, proving that her bra was removed before she died. The misrepresentation of this evidence by the prosecution is disturbing to me. The photographic evidence is very clear. When viewing the photographs it is impossible to deny the existence of the blood droplets.

Mignini's statements in court were false. How was he able to get away with this?

There was no evidence at the crime scene to show that Meredith's body was moved hours after her death. I believe, based on observations by defense experts and also given Ron Hendry's analysis, that Meredith was moved a few feet immediately after she was no longer able to fight. Rudy moved her out of the pool of blood so he could sexually assault her. While she was still breathing, her bra was pulled up to expose her breasts. At this time, blood was spraying into the air from the wound in her neck and falling back down onto the bra and her bare skin as Rudy forcefully pulled her bra off her body and sexually assaulted her. Meredith's sexual assault was not staged by Amanda and Raffaele. Rudy Guede's DNA was found inside Meredith's body. That evidence would be impossible to stage.

The prosecution also misrepresented blood evidence found on the duvet. Mignini stated the duvet must have been laid over Meredith's body long after she had died because there was no blood transferred onto it. It was implied that the blood was dry when Meredith was covered. Once again, this is simply not true. Rudy moved Meredith away from the large puddle of blood. Meredith was still bleeding profusely after Rudy moved her. Crime scene photos exhibit significant blood transfer to the duvet. There is absolutely no explanation for the prosecution's misrepresentation of the blood evidence on Meredith's body and on the duvet. This suggests an attempt to cherry pick evidence that fits one's theory and to completely ignore that which contradicts it.

The blood evidence on the floor definitively proves Meredith's body was not moved at a later time. The blood smears on the floor show in great detail that Meredith was moved during the continued attack. Ron Hendry analyzed the blood patterns on the floor and he had absolutely no doubt that Meredith was moved during the attack.

The court must have been aware of the fact that the blood evidence on the floor contradicted the prosecution's theory because the court decided to simply ignore the alleged moving of Meredith's body, deciding instead to accuse Amanda and Raffaele of coming back later to cover Meredith with the duvet. Of course, this theory is also proven false by the blood evidence on the duvet, so neither theory is supported by evidence.

Who staged the crime scene?
During his analysis, Ron Hendry uncovered an egregious error made by investigators. Ron discovered that bloodstains found under the bed (47 days after the crime) could not have been deposited when Meredith was killed because there were objects in the way.

Investigators concluded that Amanda and Raffaele threw these objects over the bloodstains to cover them as part of the staging process. Mignini used this "evidence" in his report to support his theory of a staged crime scene.

The truth is investigators created those bloodstains themselves. Photos show them ransacking the room after the murder, carelessly tossing a pair of blood-soaked boots under the bed with other footwear. When they returned to the cottage 47 days later, they removed this footwear from under the bed and found the stains—made by blood that had dripped onto the floor from the blood-soaked boots.

Amanda and Raffaele did nothing to alter the crime scene because they were not there. It looks like the only ones responsible for manipulating evidence were the investigators themselves.

Clean up

The prosecution claimed that Amanda and Raffaele not only staged the crime scene described above, but also made an effort to clean up evidence that would point to them.

The prosecution alleged that the footprints detected with luminol proved there was a clean-up effort, but of course this is false. Luminol does not prove that there was any clean-up effort. There was absolutely no proof presented in court showing that a clean up occurred. As I have stated before, luminol glows from contact with many different substances other than blood, reacting with various household cleaners, different types of soil, rust in tap water, etc. As discussed in chapter ten, prints tested with luminol all tested negative for blood. What exactly are Amanda and Raffaele being accused of cleaning up?

If luminol actually detected stains that had been cleaned up, how could the barefoot prints found with luminol still be so well defined? The cleaning process would have smeared the bare footprints, causing the prints to lose their contour. Also, there was one bare footprint inside Amanda's room that does not match Amanda or Meredith. This print has the pristine shape of a foot, proving it was not the result of a visible stain that had been cleaned. Knowing this print was never cleaned shows that the stains detected with luminol could have been deposited on the floor at any time by any of the residents or their guests. The court did disagree with the prosecution on this point, but Massei easily explains it all away by saying the prints that showed the actual shape of a foot were not cleaned up. The court believes that the shapeless stains were cleaned up and the stains that appeared as footprints weren't visible on the floor until highlighted with luminol. So according to Massei, some of the blood on the tile floor was invisible. I happen to agree with Massei that the prints were not visible. Of course, he is wrong about the blood. We know that the stains tested negative for blood and we also know that blood is not invisible. The prints were invisible because they were made by wet feet coming from the shower. Water is invisible when it dries on a tile floor; blood is not.

Another claim was made that Amanda attempted to clean up her own fingerprints from the crime scene.

Mignini had this to say regarding Amanda's fingerprints:

"It is reasonable to hypothesize that she herself felt the need to eliminate the traces of her presence from an apartment in which she lived."

At trial, the prosecutor's own fingerprint expert, Giuseppe Privitera, flatly refuted this hypothesis. He said fingerprints tend to get smudged; often it is hard to find good ones even of someone who lives at the scene of an investigation, and nothing he found at the cottage suggested that any effort had been made to remove fingerprints intentionally.

So, the prosecution was unable to provide any evidence showing there had been a clean up. Bloody shoe prints from Rudy Guede's shoes are seen going down the hall and right out the front door. How could Amanda and Raffaele clean the floor, removing all of the evidence that pointed at them, while leaving all of the evidence that pointed to Rudy completely untouched? There is no evidence whatsoever to place Amanda or Raffaele in Meredith's room at the time of the murder. No clean up of any kind was attempted in Meredith's room. This type of clean-up effort would literally be impossible.

When people commit a crime such as a murder, they usually flee the scene—getting as far away as possible—or they go to great lengths to conceal their crime. Amanda and Raffaele are accused of spending many hours cleaning the cottage after the murder. With this amount of time, you would expect to see signs of a meticulous cleaning effort. Instead, there was no evidence of any cleaning at all. The floors were left untouched. There was no cleaning done in Meredith's room and the bathroom certainly showed no signs of clean up. Simply running the water would have eliminated the blood traces found in the sink and the bidet. How could anyone look at the bathroom and insinuate that a cleaning effort took place?

Of course, the ridiculous argument is made that Amanda and Raffaele intended on leaving the blood evidence in the bathroom. Are we really supposed to believe that Amanda and Raffaele committed a brutal murder after smoking marijuana, and then, instead of getting as far away from the scene as possible, they decided to spend many hours in the cottage cleaning and devising a complicated plan to cover it up? Does anyone really believe that Amanda was cleaning the cottage and thought – "Hey, let's leave a little blood, then when I return here tomorrow to take my shower I can see the blood and become concerned, and then I can return to your house and let you know. We will pretend to discuss my concern and then we will return together and call the police"?

If Amanda and Raffaele actually took the time to think out this plan as suggested, why on earth would they want to leave potentially incriminating blood evidence? Most ridiculous of all, why would they choose to leave the footprint on the bathmat? If Raffaele actually made that print, he would have obviously known the print belonged to him. Why not just roll the bathmat up and get rid of it? Raffaele had no such concern because the footprint was not his.

When we look at what Amanda and Raffaele are accused of with regard to the alleged clean-up effort, an important question remains unanswered. If Amanda and Raffaele were actually involved, why would they try to frame Rudy Guede? If all three committed the murder, why would they lead investigators to a man who could potentially incriminate them? If Amanda and Raffaele were attempting to clean up evidence, wouldn't they attempt to clean up the evidence of all involved? The court's theory makes no sense. There is no polite way to say it: their reasoning is ludicrous.

The evidence at the crime scene shows that one person broke into the cottage and attacked Meredith Kercher. The prosecution did everything possible to find evidence that supported their theory of a group attack. When the investigation of the cottage failed to provide the evidence they hoped for, instead of changing their theory, they simply accused Amanda and Raffaele of miraculously cleaning up all of the evidence that would point to them.

Did the court honestly believe this garbage about the clean up, or did they simply ignore anything that could sway them away from their predetermined decision of guilt? It just seems impossible to me that a group of intelligent people could look at the facts presented and conclude that the prosecution had it right.

Witnesses

The prosecution had a very difficult time finding credible witnesses to support their case. This is no surprise since the prosecution's case was based on a fantasy. It would be extremely difficult to find witnesses that saw Amanda and Raffaele anywhere near the cottage on the night of the murder, because as we know, they were not there. The prosecution set out to cherry pick witnesses that could somehow support their theory. The witnesses they found turned out to be a major embarrassment. Overall, the witness search was a total failure. Witnesses that took the stand for the prosecution did nothing to help prove the guilt of Amanda Knox and Raffaele Sollecito. In fact, several aspects of their testimony actually helped prove their innocence.

This crime could have easily occurred without a single person witnessing anything at all. The murder took place inside a cottage that was not in direct view from many locations. If no one saw Rudy enter or leave the cottage, then this crime could easily have had no witnesses. There were a few key witnesses that were in the vicinity of the cottage on the night of the murder that provided vital information. It was not what they saw but what they did not see that was important. Let's take a look at the prosecution's star witnesses.

Antonio Curatolo is a homeless man who sleeps in Piazza Grimana. Curatolo turned out to be an embarrassment for the prosecution. His testimony completely backfired when at one point he actually provided an alibi for Amanda and Raffaele. Massei's determination to make Curatolo's testimony work in the motivation report led him to disregard a large portion of his testimony. Massei cherry picked what he needed in an attempt to claim that Curatolo stated he did not see Amanda and Raffaele between 11:00 and 11:30 pm.

Curatolo testified nine times that he saw Amanda and Raffaele hanging around outside from 11:30 pm to 12:00 am. He testified only once that he only saw Amanda and Raffaele around 11:00 pm. Massei ignored nine statements made by Curatolo and chose to believe the one statement that he needed to support the court's decision. Nine out of ten times, Curatolo said the exact same thing. One time he altered his statement, and that one slip was good enough for Massei.

A kiosk vendor who was doing business near Curatolo's bench contradicted his testimony. Her testimony showed how easily Curatolo became confused about each day's events. The woman had set up her kiosk near Curatolo's bench on the day in question. She stated she saw Curatolo on the morning of November 2 on the bench at 6:40 am when she opened her kiosk. Curatolo claimed that he slept in the park and didn't get up till 8:30 or 9:00 am.

Curatolo was also confused about what day he was referring to. He claimed that on the evening he saw Amanda and Raffaele, he left the piazza after he saw several buses full of young people leaving for the discos. However, there were no disco buses running that night because all of the discos were closed. This observation, along with the kiosk owner's testimony, clearly shows that Curatolo was most likely remembering a different night. His confusion suggests that he is not a credible witness.

Of course, the court decided to accept Curatolo's testimony. Well, sort of. They accepted the part they liked. They ignored the fact that Curatolo provided an alibi for Amanda and Raffaele from 9:30 pm to midnight in nine of his ten statements.

Hekuran Kokomani is an Albanian man with reported drug and alcohol problems. He testified that he saw the three suspects together on the night of the murder. Kokomani is the only person anywhere who claims he saw Amanda, Raffaele, and Rudy together on the night of the murder. He was supposed to be the prosecution's "super witness," but his testimony contained statements that quickly discredited him. Kokomani described Amanda as a girl with gaps in her teeth and mentioned he knew she had an Italian uncle. Kokomani was not considered credible; he was another embarrassment for the prosecution.

Fabio Gioffredi stated that he saw Amanda, Raffaele, Meredith, and Rudy together on October 30, 2007 between 4:30 and 5:30 pm. Raffaele's computer shows intensive human activity from 5:30 to 6:30 pm on that day. The prosecution suggested that Raffaele went out for a walk leaving his computer on. Yet computer records show intensive human activity during that exact time frame, thus refuting the prosecution's claims. Massei does not give any credibility to Gioffredi's testimony, so this most likely won't be an issue on appeal. This witness highlights the fact that the prosecution had no evidence whatsoever to show that the three suspects knew each other before the murder took place. The prosecution knew it was highly unlikely that three complete strangers met up to commit a brutal murder. They tried desperately to link the three suspects but failed miserably.

Nara Capezzali lives in a nearby apartment and claims to have heard a scream followed by the footsteps of more than one person in the street at around 11:30 pm on the night of the murder. There is no way that Nara heard a scream coming from Meredith's room. The distance from the cottage to Nara's window was simply too far. Paul Ciolino, a private investigator retained by CBS to investigate this case, conducted an unscientific but very effective test to see if the noise Nara described could actually be heard at that distance. He was able to gain access to another apartment in Nara's building. When sound tests were conducted, he was unable to make out the sounds coming from outside. The apartment windows were double glazed and there were other obstacles between the apartment building and the cottage. It was simply impossible to have heard a scream. Paul wasn't even able to say for sure if he could hear people running outside and that was at a shorter distance than the alleged scream.

The scream was allegedly so "blood curdling" that Nara did not bother to look at the time or call the police. Her daughter, who was in bed, did not even wake up, and Nara never even looked out the window. The next morning, Nara mentioned this alleged scream to no one.

Nara contradicts her own testimony and is also contradicted by other witness testimony. Three other witnesses testified having been near the cottage at the time Nara claims she heard a scream. These three witnesses were dealing with a broken-down vehicle in front of the cottage, yet none of them heard a scream.

The prosecution believed that Amanda and Raffaele were barefoot in the cottage at the time of the murder. Nara's time frame does not support the prosecution's theory. It would have been tough for Amanda and Raffaele to get their shoes on and run outside in the short time frame Nara described between the scream and the footsteps. When Nara testified, she was unaware that Amanda and Raffaele would have needed time to put shoes on. I wonder if she would have allowed for more time if she knew this information.

Nara makes multiple statements that are untrue. At 11:00 am on the day Meredith's body was discovered, she heard kids saying a girl had been killed. The problem is the murder had not even been discovered at that time. Nara also claims that she saw Amanda and Raffaele standing by the parking garage observing the cottage on the day the murder was discovered. She said there were emergency vehicles everywhere. Yet after the emergency vehicles arrived, Amanda and Raffaele were in close vicinity of the police the entire time. Amanda and Raffaele never went across the street to the parking garage during that day.

Nara Capezzali's testimony was clearly influenced by journalists. Her claims kept changing as more news was brought forth. There are just too many problems with Nara's testimony, and it must be viewed as non-credible. No one doubts that Meredith would have tried to scream.

The prosecution used Nara's testimony to establish the time of the attack. The prosecution's case relies on the time of death being pushed to much later than the defense believes it to have taken place. Even though her testimony is completely unreliable, Nara provides the time frame the prosecution required for their story to fit.

Marco Quintavalle is a store owner who testified that he saw Amanda in his store the morning after the murder. Quintavalle claimed Amanda was in the store and was showing an urgency to buy something in the cleaning section, but then left without making a purchase. The court concluded that Amanda went to Quintavalle's store and purchased bleach. Investigators checked Quintavalle's cash register receipts and found no bleach purchased on that day. The court decided to ignore this. Not only did the store register not show any bleach sold, no bleach receipt has ever been produced from searches of the cottage and/or Raffaele's apartment. In fact, there was already bleach at the cottage, so there would have been no need for Amanda to go to Quintavalle's store in the first place.

Quintavalle discredited himself on the witness stand. His testimony contradicted the witness statements he made to Inspector Orestes Volturno. The court inexplicably ignored the testimony of Inspector Volturno. Quintavalle was questioned within a day or two of the murder. Volturno did a follow-up questioning of Quintavalle on November 19, 2007. The service record makes it clear that he was shown photos of Amanda and Raffaele. After looking at the photos, Quintavalle said Amanda and Raffaele had been to his store two or so times but not on November 2, and they always came together. The record indicates that Volturno spoke with Quintavalle and then his two employees. On March 21, 2009, Volturno confirms his conversations with the witnesses at the store.

Inspector Volturno's testimony from March 21, 2009 hearing:

Question: Who did you speak to?

Inspector Volturno: Quintavalle and Chiriboga since she is his assistant and another girl whose name I don't recall now.

Question: You said previously that you had photographs of Amanda and Raffaele.

Inspector Volturno: That's right.

Question: And you showed them to the people who were inside the shop?

Inspector Volturno: Yes.

Question: Therefore both the owner and his assistants.

Inspector Volturno: Yes.

Question: You said that you asked the manager of the business if he had seen the two defendants.

Inspector Volturno: Yes, exactly.

Question: What was his exact response?

Inspector Volturno: He said that Raffaele was a regular client whilst Amanda was seen on a couple of occasions in Raffaele's company.

Inspector Volturno explicitly asked Quintavalle whether he recognized the photographs of Amanda Knox and Raffaele Sollecito and whether he had seen them buy bleach in a period close to the murder. Quintavalle only recognized Amanda Knox as the girl whom he had seen entering the shop on a couple of occasions, always in the company of Raffaele Sollecito. He made absolutely no mention to investigators regarding the presence of Amanda Knox in his shop on the morning after the murder.

The first time Quintavalle stated Amanda was in his shop on the morning of the murder was almost a year later, following contact with a reporter which ended up getting him on television. Just like Nara Capezzali, Marco Quintavalle was influenced by journalists.

Quintavalle made several other claims further confirming his lack of credibility. He stated that Amanda was wearing a cap, a scarf, and a grey jacket. Quintavalle went on to state that he only saw the side of Amanda's face. On another occasion, Quintavalle claimed it was Amanda's blue eyes that he remembered. How did Quintavalle see Amanda's eyes when he'd earlier claimed to have seen only the side of her face?

Quintavalle's description of Amanda's coat was unconfirmed. No grey coat was found in Amanda's wardrobe, and no other witness ever saw Amanda in a grey coat.

Quintavalle's employee Ana Marina Chiriboga was asked in October 2008 if she had seen Amanda on November 2, 2007. Chiriboga said she had not, and she reiterated this observation in court on June 26, 2009.

Some will call Quintavalle an outright liar. Others will accuse him of committing perjury. I'll hold off on those accusations and say that Quintavalle was mistaken with regard to what he saw. Marco Quintavalle has been completely discredited and this should be noted in the appeal.

A group of Meredith's friends from the UK testified for the prosecution. The prosecution went to a lot of trouble and expense to bring in witnesses who'd make unfavorable comments about Amanda. These witnesses would testify that Amanda's behavior after the murder came across as insensitive. The most notable part of their testimony isn't what they said—it's what they didn't say.

None of these witnesses ever heard Amanda say anything negative to or about Meredith. There was no testimony mentioning Amanda ever acting angry, showing rage, or even raising her voice. None of the witnesses spoke of being intimidated by Amanda, and there was no testimony stating that Amanda ever attempted to intimidate anyone else in their presence. Amanda never stole anything from anyone, never lied to anyone, never intimidated anyone, and never yelled at anyone. In fact, there was no testimony that Amanda had ever even raised her voice slightly.

Not one witness described any behavior that could possibly be considered hostile or aggressive, much less violent.

Frank Sfarzo reported on one aspect of this testimony that was alarming to me. According to Frank, the testimony that Meredith's friends provided was almost identical, as if they had been coached.

A vehicle stalled in front of the cottage on the night of the murder. A serviceman testified that he received a call from the owners of the vehicle at around 10:30 pm and that he arrived to service the stalled vehicle at around 11:20 pm.

The court completely ignored testimony concerning the stalled vehicle. This seems to be the standard procedure of the court for any information contradicting their theory.

The owners of the vehicle testified that it took thirty minutes or more for the serviceman to arrive. Service records show it took twenty minutes to assign the service call to a serviceman and twenty more minutes to drive to the location of the stalled vehicle. So the serviceman arrived at 11:20 to 11:25 pm per witness testimony and the repair records. All involved said it took about 15 minutes to repair the vehicle. The vehicle's owners left the scene as soon as the repair was completed, around 11:35 to 11:40 pm. There was no witness testimony of any activity at the cottage from 10:30 pm until 11:35–11:40 pm.

This testimony is critical because these witnesses saw nothing at the cottage at the time the court suggested the murder occurred. The court ignored the testimony. The witness testimony regarding the time frame was confirmed by the repairman. According to this testimony, there was no activity at the cottage from 10:30 pm until 11:35–11:40 pm.

This testimony supports the defense's argument that the murder occurred at an earlier time. When the vehicle broke down in front of the cottage, the murder had already been committed and Rudy Guede had already fled the scene.

Contamination

When viewing crime scene videos detailing evidence collection at the cottage, it quickly becomes apparent that proper procedures were not followed. You needn't be an expert to understand this, as you can see egregious errors being made in the videos. There was minimal physical evidence in this case, leaving little room for error when it came to proper collection. Unfortunately, investigators neglected to follow even the most basic of procedures. I cannot help but wonder how a trained group of professionals could behave so carelessly at a time when they should have been at their best. I recall a comment I saw posted on an online discussion board where an Italian gentleman stated he had the utmost respect for the Italian authorities, but he was deeply disturbed at how this case was investigated. He wanted to know why a team of well-trained investigators entered the cottage and decided to act like children playing in a sand box. I do not know if we will ever find an answer to this question. One thing, however, is certain: the actions taken by those that were assigned to investigate this murder caused irreparable damage to two completely innocent people.

There were many instances of unprofessional behavior observed in the crime scene videos. Most of these observations pertain to improper evidence collection, but investigators are also seen laughing it up and, at one point, an investigator even takes his own picture in the bathroom mirror. I was surprised to see this behavior at the scene of a horrific murder. On another occasion, I observed what I would call peculiar behavior. One of the investigators removes a mop from the hall closet to be examined. She then takes what appears to be gift wrap from the closet and wraps the mop handle in gift wrap. I am not sure how gift wrap owned by the residents of the cottage would serve as protection, let alone the fact that the mop head remained exposed. After gift wrapping the mop handle, the investigator walks around the cottage, taking the mop into Meredith's room and then back into the hall. Why would any trained investigator carry possible evidence into the murder room and then back out? She not only risked contamination from the mop head, she also caused unnecessary foot traffic. I admit that I point out this one instance simply because I feel that it was extremely odd, but unfortunately, there are many more examples that can be pointed out showing how contamination could have occurred. I mentioned above how the investigator caused unnecessary foot traffic. I will discuss why foot traffic was so important, but first I want to discuss the importance of the investigators' gloves.

One of the easiest ways to avoid contamination is to change your gloves often. There is no video whatsoever showing any of the investigators changing gloves. In fact, you can view investigators collecting multiple samples with no breaks in the video footage. In this chapter, I will highlight some of the errors that occurred in the investigation.

I will begin with Patrizia Stefanoni collecting a blood sample from the wall in the murder room. Crime scene video shows Stefanoni swabbing a blood marking on the wall. As she swabs the blood, you can clearly see Stefanoni turn the swab around. There is a clear view showing blood on the swab that was collected from the wall; when Stefanoni turns the swab around, her thumb is pressing up against the area of the swab containing the blood sample.

Stefanoni uses both sides of the swab to collect the sample. While she is swabbing the sample, she is also smearing blood all over her glove. This wouldn't be a problem if she changed her gloves between samples, but as we can see, Stefanoni neglects to do that. Many samples are collected while wearing the same pair of gloves, causing possible contamination to every sample collected. The sample from the wall should have been collected using an instrument such as a pair of tweezers to hold the swab. Her glove shouldn't have made contact with the swab at all. At one point, Stefanoni actually has the proper instrument in her hand but she does not use it. She is seen collecting a sample from Meredith's door, holding the swab with her gloved fingers even though she has the tweezers in the same hand. She knows she is supposed to use the tweezers or she wouldn't have had them with her in the first place.

It appears the only time investigators took their gloves off was when they were leaving the cottage. Video footage captured a dirty pair of gloves discarded on the floor in the kitchen. These gloves can be seen in the video taken November 3, 2007. The gloves are extremely discolored, looking like they had been used to collect many samples. They appear to have been thrown on the floor as an investigator was heading out the front door. Why would an investigator throw dirty gloves on the floor instead of properly disposing of them?

It was disturbing to see the mess that was made of the cottage early on. Investigators trashed the cottage in early November, and then came back on December 18, 2007 to

collect more evidence and test the cottage with luminol.
Meredith's mattress had been moved to the living room,
and everything in her room was thrown in large piles on
the bed frame. No effort of any kind was made to
organize items left in the murder room. We are supposed
to believe that while everything in Meredith's room was
tossed around and the room left in total disarray, the
clasp, found in the same room, was at no risk of
contamination. Of course, this is completely ridiculous.
Evidence in the cottage was compromised long before the
December visit. Throwing dirty gloves on the floor is one
example showing brazen disregard for contamination.

Why was the floor so important?
The floor of the cottage became a very important aspect
of this case because key pieces of evidence that the
prosecution attempted to attribute to Amanda and
Raffaele were found on the floor. Evidence was also
found on the floor that was attributed to Rudy Guede.
The shoe print evidence attributed to Rudy cannot be
refuted. Rudy's shoes deposited prints set in Meredith's
blood on the floor. We have visual proof that these prints
were made by Rudy's shoes. We also have confirmation
that the prints were made in Meredith's blood. Sloppy
evidence collection throughout the cottage would have no
effect on this evidence.

The same cannot be said for the evidence attributed to
Amanda and Raffaele. The bra clasp evidence and the
stains found with luminol were severely compromised by

the negligence of the investigators. The bra clasp evidence attributed to Raffaele was not visual. The evidence was based on the discovery of his DNA on the metal hook of the clasp. As we know, there was DNA of at least six people on the clasp. The clasp was found on the floor. DNA was tracked all around the cottage by investigators. The clasp, lying on the floor for 47 days prior to its collection, was highly vulnerable to contamination. When the clasp was finally collected, multiple investigators handled the clasp with dirty gloves, passing it around like it was a prize.

The stains revealed with luminol were not only severely compromised by the foot traffic in the cottage, but were also susceptible to further contamination from having been collected with dirty gloves. Any DNA results gathered from the luminol stains are thus completely unreliable.

There is no doubt that improper use of gloves and shoe covers caused contamination of evidence on the floor throughout the entire crime scene. Investigators put shoe covers on before they entered the cottage. The problem is they never changed shoe covers when they walked from room to room. They're even seen coming and going from the cottage wearing their shoe covers, tracking in additional contamination from outside. The shoe covers actually work as a sort of dust mop. This would mean that all of the DNA throughout the cottage would have quickly been spread from room to room. Shoe covers are designed to protect floors from shoe contamination. This means that they keep dirt from transferring to the floor from the shoe. However, any dirt on the floor will adhere to the bottom of the shoe covers. The covers quickly become dirty.

At one point an investigator is seen standing outside on the balcony of the cottage wearing shoe covers. This would mean that he was in the hall across from Meredith's door and decided to walk outside for some fresh air. Where else did he walk? How many people's DNA did he pick up on those shoe covers? Was he one of the investigators that kicked the bra clasp? Did he step on the bra clasp? The clasp was left on the floor for forty-seven days. The clasp was seen in several different areas on the floor before it ended up under a dirty rug. Did this investigator kick it there? How many investigators were in the house wearing shoe covers? The investigator can also be seen, still wearing his gloves, holding onto the railing of the balcony. Did these investigators ever change their gloves? Whose DNA was on the railing or the door knob of the door leading to the balcony? When you don't follow proper procedure, contamination is guaranteed. Procedures are put into place for a reason, and those procedures need to be followed.

The damage caused by the investigators was bad enough to destroy evidence, but they were not the first ones to contaminate the floor. The first contamination occurred in a very innocent fashion. When Amanda came home the morning of November 2, 2007 to take her shower, she walked on the floor with bare feet. Her feet would have been wet from the shower. Her wet feet would be highly likely to alter evidence on the tile floor. Amanda and Raffaele would later return to the cottage to discuss what Amanda had seen. This would have not only caused more foot traffic but would also have compromised evidence on the floor outside of Meredith's door when Raffaele made the attempt to break her door down. Soon after that, the floor would be subject to more foot traffic. Two postal police officers entered the cottage. Filomena, Paola, Marco, and Luca also walked throughout the cottage. If we add it up, that is a total of sixteen feet repeatedly walking up and down the narrow hallway before the murder was even discovered. Then the door was broken down, causing even more disturbance to the floor in front of Meredith's door. Shortly after that, paramedics arrived to examine Meredith.

Giuliano Mignini also contributed possible contamination. Mignini can be seen arriving at the cottage. Mignini enters the cottage with police woman Lorena Zugarini. Mignini and Zugarini never break stride once they reach the entrance and don't stop to put on shoe covers before entering the cottage.

Mignini is later seen outside the downstairs flat entrance when Zugarini kicks open the window so that the door can be opened. By this time, Mignini has put on a pair of shoe covers. Mignini is also seen outside the upstairs flat entrance and out in the parking lot wearing the shoe covers. Mignini neglected to put shoe covers on when he first entered the cottage. Once he decided to put on a pair of shoe covers, he never changed them as he walked everywhere around the cottage and its surrounding property. Mignini's poor procedures may have contributed to the contamination.

Investigators can be seen both inside and outside the cottage with their shoe covers on throughout the crime scene video. Shoe covers cannot protect against contamination if you do not use them properly. Investigators are supposed to change shoe covers as they move from one room to the next. They certainly should not have been walking in and out of the cottage wearing the same pairs of shoe covers. Improper procedures contaminated much of the floor evidence. The prosecution utterly ignored the possibility of contamination as the evidence was presented at trial.

What about the mixed DNA?

Evidence collection in the bathroom was also a serious problem. Gioia Brocci, photographic agent of the Questura of Perugia, collected the evidence samples in the bathroom shared by Amanda and Meredith. Three of the samples showed Amanda's DNA mixed with Meredith's blood. The prosecution has tried to insinuate that these findings are incriminating.

Meredith's blood was visible in several areas in the bathroom. I believe that Rudy Guede used the bathroom to quickly clean himself up. When he did this he left behind small amounts of Meredith's blood. As stated above, three of these samples were mixed with Amanda's DNA. This is completely understandable because Amanda used the bathroom daily.

To put this in perspective, think about your own bathroom. Swabbing your bathroom sink in the bathroom that you use daily would unquestionably yield your DNA. When Brocci collected the samples from the bathroom she swabbed large surface areas to clean up the blood. When doing this she also wiped up Amanda's DNA in the process. When collecting samples, Brocci actually advanced the mixing process. She used the swabs like a cleaning rag.

It was unknown at the time, but the drop of blood on the faucet belonged to Amanda. It is very important to note that this blood was not mixed with any other DNA. The small drop of blood on the faucet most likely came from an irritated ear piercing.

The crime scene video clearly shows the samples being improperly collected in the bathroom. Brocci wiped Amanda's drop of blood off the faucet before she collected the other samples on the sink, toilet, wall, and bidet. Brocci kept her thumb down and rubbed her thumb repeatedly over the sample. When doing this, she undoubtedly got some of Amanda's blood on her glove.

Brocci did not change her gloves after she collected each sample. When she collected the next sample after the faucet, she once again put the same thumb down into the sample that she was collecting. Keep in mind— though it was unknown at the time—the sample from the faucet contained Amanda's blood. She had now repeatedly rubbed her thumb in Amanda's blood and then onto the next sample.

When Brocci collected the samples from the sink and the bidet, she used a wiping motion and wiped multiple surfaces with the same swab. She was collecting Amanda's DNA from Amanda's own bathroom as she was collecting Meredith's blood samples. Not only was she collecting Amanda's residual DNA, she was mixing it together with Meredith's blood.

The crime scene videos clearly show that the mixed DNA that was collected from the bathroom is not incriminating in any way. The DNA samples can be used to show that Meredith's blood was present in the bathroom. The evidence can also be used to show who possibly used the bathroom. The fact that these samples are mixed means nothing.

Brocci advanced the mixing process with her evidence collection procedures. She wiped large surfaces when she collected the samples. She did not change gloves after collecting Amanda's drop of blood from the faucet or after collecting any of the other samples. Both of these procedures undoubtedly mixed the DNA.

Substrate Control Tests

Given the significance the prosecution has attributed to the mixed DNA samples, it is unfortunate that investigators didn't bother to perform substrate control tests. This testing is done to determine if contamination occurred. Samples are collected in areas other than the areas where evidence samples were collected. These would be areas close to the location of the sample. For instance, if you collected a blood sample on a wall, you would also swab an area on the same wall where there was no blood. If DNA is mixed with the blood sample and that same DNA was also present on the wall, then it could be concluded that the DNA mix was due to DNA that was present on the wall long before the blood was deposited there. This testing would have been very useful in the bathroom. If other areas in the bathroom that were free from blood were swabbed, we could determine if Amanda's DNA was present in the room before the blood was deposited there. Unfortunately, no control testing was done. Logic tells us that Amanda's DNA would be present in her own bathroom. With no testing to prove otherwise, it must be concluded that Amanda's DNA was present in her own bathroom before any crime ever took place.

Given the crime scene investigators were met with at the cottage, substrate control tests were a must. Sadly, no control testing of any kind was performed. The errors committed by the investigators were very damaging to Amanda and Raffaele. Proper testing would have decisively shown their innocence. Amanda and Raffaele wouldn't have been put on trial if the evidence in this case had been properly collected and analyzed.

15

Giuliano Mignini

I do not pretend to know Giuliano Mignini. I cannot judge his character by his personal life nor do I have any interest in doing so. The information that is available to the public regarding prosecutor Mignini is more than sufficient to show that he had no business being in the courtroom prosecuting the Meredith Kercher murder case.

Mignini has been convicted in Florence of abusing his official powers. This abuse of power took place while Mignini was investigating the death of Dr. Francesco

Narducci in relation to the Monster of Florence case. Mignini has been sentenced to 16 months in prison. Normal procedure in Italian criminal justice allows him to live his life and carry on—business as usual—until his appeal is heard. This freedom also allows him to continue to prosecute cases. Mignini described the charges against him as technical and difficult to understand. But the charges are not confusing at all: Mignini abused the power of his office.

Mignini was convicted of illegally investigating journalists who had criticized him. The court found that Mignini had targeted Italian journalists Vincenzo Tessandori, Gennaro De Stefano, and Roberto Fiasconaro because they had criticized his investigation of Narducci's death.

Mignini was also convicted on two separate charges of ordering illegal investigations. These illegal investigations targeted the Florentine ex-police chief Giuseppe De Donno as well as two officials of the Viminale (the Ministry of the Interior in Rome), including Roberto Sgalla, former director of the office of external affairs.

These investigations were unlawful because they involved illegal wiretaps. Mignini also created investigative files for his targets without proper approval. The court determined that his investigations were designed to "harass and intimidate" people who had criticized him or Chief Inspector Michele Giuttari for their conduct during the Narducci investigation.

Mignini was also charged with "aiding and abetting," but was acquitted of that charge. He was accused of informing Giuttari that he was being investigated for doctoring the recording of a wiretap in an attempt to frame one of his targets.

The charges against Mignini are serious. Some members of the media have reported that these charges are simply administrative. This is not the case. Mignini was given a sixteen-month prison sentence, six months more than the prosecutor asked for. However, he is unlikely to see jail time and his sentence is suspended while his case is on appeal.

Unfortunately, Mignini will most likely never spend any time in jail. However, his career is in serious jeopardy. If his conviction is upheld, he will be removed from public office and will no longer be allowed to serve as a prosecutor or judge. His career will be over.

What was the Monster of Florence case?

There was a series of murders that occurred in Italy during the 1970s and 80s. The perpetrator of the murders was given the name "Monster of Florence" by the press. Young couples who were parked in remote areas—presumably to have sex—were shot and the bodies of the female victims mutilated. Crime experts believed that the perpetrator was a Jack the Ripper type killer. Mignini got involved in the Monster of Florence case while investigating the death of Dr. Francesco Narducci, whose drowned corpse was found in a lake near Perugia.

Mignini was far from an expert in these types of murders. He was a conspiracy theorist that liked to dream up wild fantasies. Mignini's theory was that the young couples were murdered so that their body parts could be used in rituals performed by satanic cults. Mignini believed that Dr. Narducci had belonged to this cult, but he'd become a security risk, so other cult members decided to kill him and make it look like an accident or suicide.

His theory was challenged by author Douglas Preston and his writing partner Mario Spezi. Douglas and Mario decided to write a book about the Monster of Florence. They both agreed that Mignini's theory was ridiculous. Mario Spezi stated so publicly. Mignini didn't like being challenged. Mignini had Spezi's office ransacked and he bugged his car. Mignini interrogated Preston and forced him to leave the country. Mignini arrested Spezi and threw him into jail. After three weeks in solitary confinement for no reason whatsoever, a judge ordered Spezi released despite Mignini's objections.

Mario Spezi's arrest drew the attention of CPJ, The Committee to Protect Journalists, an independent, nonpartisan organization dedicated to defending the rights of journalists worldwide. CPJ released a letter in regard to Spezi's arrest.

Mignini interrogated Douglas Preston. He accused him of being an accessory to murder in the Monster of Florence case. He told him that he would never see his family again. He threatened that Preston would go to an Italian prison. Preston says that his knees were shaking.

He could hardly walk when he stood up. He was terrified. Mignini successfully forced Preston to leave Italy. To read the full account of Giuliano Mignini's involvement in the case, check out *The Monster of Florence* by Douglas Preston.

Mignini's imagination goes to work again
When Giuliano Mignini began investigating the Meredith Kercher murder case, he developed a theory that the crime started out as a sadistic sex game that turned in to a brutal murder when Meredith refused to participate. His fantasy of a group sex game gone wrong was based on nothing more than his imagination.

As the investigation of Meredith's murder progressed, investigators discovered evidence—evidence that is discussed in great detail in this book. Mignini's fantasy should have deteriorated with the discovery of this evidence, but it seemed to have little effect on him.

Mignini should have backed up and looked at the case from a fresh perspective. He had plenty of evidence to convict Rudy Guede. He had no evidence to convict Amanda and Raffaele. Even with the truth staring him in the face, Mignini refused to rethink his original theory. He was convinced that Meredith Kercher was murdered in a group sex game. He had already told his fantasy to the press. Bold statements were made that the crime had been solved. There was no turning back now. Mignini's fragile reputation was more important than the lives of Amanda Knox and Raffaele Sollecito.

To help reinforce his claims, Miginini ran a smear campaign against Amanda Knox. Mignini's office released misinformation and outright lies to the public. He continued his tactics even while under investigation. He successfully destroyed Amanda Knox in the court of public opinion. She was considered guilty long before her trial ever started. This was largely due to Mignini's use of the media to spread lies and misinformation. When all was said and done, Giuliano Mignini succeeded in convicting two innocent people.

An attempt to silence those who disagree

Mignini makes an effort to attack anyone who disagrees with him. Spezi and Preston simply disagreed with Mignini's view of a crime; Mignini tried to destroy their lives. Mignini's tactics didn't change during Amanda and Raffaele's trial. Once again, Mignini attacked his critics. He filed defamation charges against several people who publicly dared to disagree with him. He even filed charges against the defense lawyers. Mignini attempted to use these lawsuits to embarrass Amanda and Raffaele. He has attacked their families as well as their lawyers, and he used these lawsuits to put fear into the minds of journalists in hopes of silencing them.

Here is a list of Mignini's lawsuits. The count stands at eleven. It would be twelve, but one of Mignini's targets recently passed away. Who's next on his list?

1. Amanda Knox: Amanda was charged with defamation of the police for claiming she was hit on the back of the head during her illegal interrogation. The wrongful conviction wasn't enough for Mignini.

2. Edda Mellas and Curt Knox were served papers just before the verdict was announced against their daughter. Amanda's parents were charged with slander for simply for repeating court testimony. During an interview, they told a reporter that Amanda testified in court that she had been hit on the back of the head. They merely repeated the court testimony of their daughter, and for that, Mignini slapped a lawsuit on them. Is he trying to keep them from visiting their daughter in prison? Is he really that cold-hearted?

3. Curt Knox (see Edda)

4. *The West Seattle Herald*: Mignini filed defamation charges this time because Herald reporter Steve Shay quoted other people as saying Mignini was "mentally unstable." Mignini actually filed a lawsuit against a newspaper in Seattle, Washington, because they hurt his feelings.

5. Joe Cottonwood from joecottonwood.com. Take a look at Joe's website. Joe is a fiction writer. Joe doesn't even like Amanda Knox. He was simply voicing his opinion about the case. Why was Mignini

threatened by him? Here is Joe's quote that won him the honors of a Mignini lawsuit:

"The Meredith Kercher murder is one of those mirrors that reflects the prejudices of whoever is looking into it. There is no physical evidence and no credible motive, and yet an egotistical prosecutor is blaming Amanda Knox anyway. In the USA, this would only happen if she were black. Perhaps partying American college kids are so hated in Italy that Amanda will be treated as blacks are treated in the USA, and she will be convicted not because of the evidence but because of general resentment of shallow rich Americans. Personally, from what I've read I don't like Amanda Knox. She sounds spoiled, naive, and shallow. But that's not a crime. I loathe the prosecutor, who has a counterpart in every city in the USA - a preening, intellectually dishonest bully who cares more about making newspaper headlines than in serving justice. It's the same all over the world. Power and prejudice are the enemies of justice."

6. Luciano Ghirga (attorney for Amanda Knox)

7. Luca Maori (attorney for Raffaele Sollecito)

8. Giangavino Sulas (journalist for *Oggi* magazine)

9. The director and editor of *Oggi* magazine

10. Mario Spezi: Spezi is an Italian journalist who co-wrote *The Monster of Florence* with journalist and author Doug Preston. Mignini continues to torment Spezi for disagreeing with him.

11. Francesca Bene: Bene, an Italian reporter, said Knox had, in her opinion, advanced her cause by making clear what police had not previously conceded—that Knox thought she was being a helpful witness when in fact police were targeting her as a suspect and should have told her so. Mignini didn't like hearing the truth.

12. Gabriella Carlizzi: Carlizzi was a psychic. Mignini charged Carlizzi with defamation multiple times. Doug Preston says that Mignini used Carlizzi as a witness in the Monster of Florence case. Gabriella Carlizzi recently passed away. So our list currently stands at eleven . . . unless Mignini plans on going after Gabriella's family.

Keeping tabs on your enemies

Mignini actually keeps blacklists, reportedly to target his enemies. Mignini's list of enemies was detailed in *Panorama* magazine. During the investigation leading up to Mignini's conviction, the authorities confiscated his computer. When the computer was analyzed, investigators found Mignini's blacklist. The list allegedly included the names of parliamentarians, ministers, and journalists.

Panorama reported that Mignini created a file he called "Attacks to Remember." Within that file was another file titled "Orgy of Attacks Following the Arrest of Spezi; an index of newspapers: Libero, Il Giornale, Oggi." The main file also included a long list of people "to remember" that contained names of prominent judges involved in the Monster case, as well a long list of politicians including former mayor of Florence Leonardo Domenici, the deputy mayor Michele Venturo, and the Minister of the Environment Altero Matteoli. What did those three officials have in common? They all signed a petition protesting Spezi's incarceration. Creating blacklists for the sole purpose of attacking enemies is not the behavior you would expect from a prosecutor. In fact, this behavior is very dangerous.

Giuliano Mignini's satanic theories are rejected by a judge

In relation to the Monster of Florence case, Mignini indicted twenty people and charged them with the concealment of Dr. Francesco Narducci's murder. Mignini's ridiculous theory was dismissed, and now the twenty people harassed by him are free of all charges and can finally move past this unfortunate event.

Judge Paolo Micheli threw out the case against all twenty accused, having found no solid evidence to back up even Mignini's claim that Narducci was murdered, much less the victim of a satanic cult.

Mignini originally argued that Meredith Kercher's murder had a demonic motive. If he is able to work long enough, maybe he'll eventually get the satanic case he's always dreamt of. But if justice has a voice in Italy, Mignini's conviction will be confirmed on appeal and he won't have the chance to destroy any more lives.

Italy is to blame for allowing Giuliano Mignini to continue prosecuting cases. As we know, he was on trial for abuse of office while prosecuting Amanda and Raffaele's trial. He shouldn't have been anywhere near this case. He has repeatedly shown his paranoia by slapping defamation lawsuits on those that disagree with him. He's made every attempt possible to destroy the lives of two innocent people. He should no longer have the power to prosecute. Even after his conviction for abuse of office, Mignini still holds on to his power. And that is unacceptable.

The fact that Mignini is allowed to prosecute more cases is beyond ludicrous, and the news surrounding Mignini only gets worse as time goes on. We now know that Mignini will be involved in Amanda and Raffaele's appeal. Due to the nature of the crime, Italian law provides the opportunity for prosecutors from the trial that secured the conviction to assist the lead prosecutor during the appeal. As long as Mignini is involved, I have little faith that Amanda and Raffaele will ever have the chance at getting a fair trial.

Misconduct

mis·con·duct: wrongful, improper, or unlawful conduct
motivated by premeditated or intentional purpose

When three innocent people were arrested in Perugia,
Italy, for the murder of Meredith Kercher, a horrible
mistake occurred. When the actual killer was brought into
custody, the mistake should have been corrected
immediately. The innocent should have been freed, and
the man responsible should have received proper
punishment for his heinous crime.

When authorities refused to correct their mistake, they committed the most egregious act of misconduct observed in this case. Many other acts of misconduct were committed both before and after the wrongful arrests. We all know from the time we are very young that the only way to cover up a lie is to tell more lies. This is exactly what happened in this case. We have already discussed the acts of misconduct leading up to the wrongful arrests. We know Amanda Knox was illegally interrogated and we know there was an extreme rush to judgment by the authorities. This chapter will take a look at the acts of misconduct by those in power in an attempt to justify their decisions and cover up the truth.

In any civilized nation, people are given a fair trial when they are accused of a crime. For a fair trial, there are fundamental guidelines that must be followed. In this case, the prosecution made it completely impossible for Amanda and Raffaele to receive a fair trial, primarily by withholding evidence from the defense. Of course, this was necessary because a fair trial would most certainly have exposed the truth they hoped to hide.

What evidence was withheld? The prosecution failed to disclose the electronic data files (.fsa files) of the DNA evidence to the defense. What are .fsa files and why are they important? Technical bulletin 40-035 from Chromosomal Laboratories, Inc., is a checklist of what the laboratory is expected to provide, and it states:

"Copies of all data files used and created in the course of performing tests and analyzing data in this case, including .fsa files, if applicable. These files should include all data necessary to independently reanalyze the raw data."

These files would provide a means for an independent expert to analyze the data collected by the prosecution's expert. Chris Halkides has written extensively about this topic in his blog, *View-from-Wilmington*. In his blog, Chris quotes Professor Dan Krane:

"The biggest concern that I personally have regarding this case is the refusal of the prosecution to provide the defense with a copy of the electronic data that underlies the DNA test results— that is virtually unheard of world-wide today and it would be especially important to review that data in a case such as this which seems to involve such low-level samples."

Why would this information be withheld from the defense? What did the prosecution have to hide? We all know what they had to hide: Patrizia Stefanoni's lab work was not properly conducted.

The defense asked the judge to correct this obvious act of misconduct. Raffaele's attorney, Giulia Bongiorno, told the judge the following:

"My client has been denied his right to adequate representation."

The defense suggested a mistrial. The judge may not have seen the need for a mistrial, but one would have thought he would have ordered the files released to the defense immediately.

So what happened when the court was made aware of the fact that the prosecution withheld evidence? The court did order the prosecution to turn over some files to the defense. It was at this time that the defense discovered that Stefanoni lied about blood tests. This will be discussed further a little later in this chapter.

Despite the court order, guess what the defense never received? That's right—the defense is *still* waiting to see the electronic data files of the DNA evidence. To this day, these files have never been released by the prosecution. The .fsa files are not the only evidence that has been withheld. The prosecution also failed to produce the recording of Amanda's interrogation. It is no surprise that crucial evidence that would quickly crumble the prosecution's case has simply disappeared.

One way to make sure evidence never sees a courtroom is to simply destroy it. This was the case with the personal computers of Amanda, Raffaele, and Meredith.

During the preliminary investigation, investigators seized the computers. At some during inspection, the computers were damaged. This damage has never been properly explained. The electronic boards of all three hard disks were damaged to the point that no data can be recovered.

The destruction of this evidence was crucial for Amanda's case. Her computer contained many photographs of her and Meredith enjoying each other's company. These photographs would have undermined the prosecution's attempts to discredit their friendship.

The court appeared to make an attempt to recover the lost data. The court appointed Professor Massimo Bernaschi to investigate the damage caused to the computers and to recover data. Bernaschi found that each computer had sustained damage to the printed circuit board. How this happened to all three computers is unknown. It's been suggested that the computers may have been improperly connected to a power source or connected to the wrong kind of power source, causing a short circuit.

The decision was made to send the computers to a company specializing in data recovery. The company was able to recover the data from the computers owned by Meredith and Raffaele, but was unsuccessful with Amanda's computer. The computer was then sent to two more companies that specialize in data recovery. Both had the same conclusion as the first. The last company to examine the computer suggested that the computer's manufacturer, in this case Toshiba, was the only remaining chance of recovering the data from Amanda's hard drive. The defense petitioned the court to allow

Toshiba to examine Amanda's computer. Amanda's
family even offered to pay for the cost of the
examination, but the court denied the request. What
credible reason could the court possibly have had to deny
this request? How was Amanda's computer damaged to
the point that three different companies that specialize in
data recovery were completely unsuccessful in recovering
any data at all? When did this damage occur? Why did
the court refuse to let the manufacturer examine the
computer?

We have now seen how evidence was withheld to
prevent its being seen by the court, and we have also seen
evidence destroyed to that same end. We will now
discuss how evidence was prevented from being seen by
the court by neglecting to test it.

This evidence pertains to a possible semen stain
found on Meredith's pillow (under her body) at the
murder scene.

We know from examining the crime scene videos that
the evidence collection was sloppy. We've discussed the
likelihood of contamination. The sloppy evidence
collection alone would be considered misconduct, but the
complete failure to analyze evidence crucial to the crime
was another egregious act of misconduct. This goes far
beyond sloppy collection procedures. This type of
negligence destroys innocent lives.

There is absolutely no excuse for this stain to remain
untested. Raffaele's defense will make the request on

appeal that testing be done on this stain. The court stated in the first trial that the stain could not be dated because Meredith was sexually active, and so there was no reason to test it.

Forensics expert Francesco Vinci found this same substance smeared in one of Rudy's shoe prints on the pillow. This proves the substance was wet at the time of the murder and must have been deposited on the pillow at that time. Professor Vinci made this discovery using Crimescope, the same technique used to prove that all of the shoeprints in the murder room belonged to Rudy Guede.

Why wasn't this substance tested to begin with? The investigators were presented with a murder with sexual assault and they neglected to test a substance that appeared to be semen. If this substance tests positive for semen and it is attributed to Rudy, the prosecution's entire theory would be false. There is absolutely no excuse to neglect testing a possible semen stain at the scene of a brutal rape and murder. No excuse at all.

In relation to the possible semen stain, both defense teams are asking for further investigation of Mario Joseph Alessi, a prison inmate that claims to have had confidential conversations with Rudy Guede. During these conversations, Rudy allegedly discusses sexual acts that could have contributed the stains left on the pillow. The defense argues that Alessi's statements contain details of the crime that only Guede would have known. These details would confirm that these discussions actually took place. It is imperative that these stains be tested on appeal.

Amanda's clothing is another item of evidence that needs to be discussed in this chapter, because I feel the negligence observed with regard to this evidence is another act of misconduct. The misconduct observed pertains to failure of investigators to properly collect and analyze Amanda's clothing that was left in her bedroom at the cottage.

Amanda stated that she returned to the cottage the morning of November 2 to take a shower. She stated that she changed into clean clothes and left her clothes from the previous day lying on her bed.

The police would claim that the sweatshirt Amanda wore on the day of the murder was missing. This missing sweatshirt would become part of the evidence list against Amanda as reviewed by the Supreme Court.

During a later search of the cottage, Amanda's sweatshirt and the rest of her clothing were found on her bed—left there when she showered and changed into clean clothing—exactly as she said. The sweatshirt matched Filomena's description of the clothing worn by Amanda on the day of the murder. All of Amanda's clothes from that day were tested and all tested negative for blood. How was it possible for evidence in plain sight to be completely overlooked? There is no excuse for this negligence. The sweatshirt was used against Amanda by the Italian Supreme Court to show culpability. This damage could not be erased by the discovery of the sweatshirt months later.

You have HIV

Shortly after Amanda was imprisoned, she received devastating news from the prison doctor. Amanda was told that she was HIV positive. This was discussed in chapter five with regard to how poorly this story was handled in the media.

I was personally disgusted when I learned the details of this lie. Amanda was already under extreme stress when this lie was told to her. I cannot imagine the devastation and loneliness Amanda must have felt at that moment. She was left to deal with this news alone in her prison cell. Amanda would show strength and courage in handling this situation.

I feel Amanda's response in this deep time of sorrow shows her true character. She was looking out for the well being of others when she sat down and wrote a list of her past sexual partners. Of course, this is what the authorities were looking for when they devised this plan. This was just another attempt to destroy Amanda's character. When you look at the list Amanda created, you see that her sex life was very similar to many people her age. There was certainly nothing in the list to suggest that Amanda's sex life was anything but ordinary.

Telling Amanda the HIV lie was not the only act of misconduct concerning this matter. The information obtained from Amanda's list was later leaked to the

European press. We've seen how the media assassinated the character of Amanda Knox. This was a perfect example of that. Not only was this leak immoral, it was a violation of Italian law.

There have been many lies told throughout the course of this case, but who is telling these lies? For nearly three years now it's been reported that Amanda Knox and Raffaele Sollecito told numerous lies and repeatedly changed their alibis. If you look past the media spin and the guilter movement online, you can see the truth more clearly. The most egregious lies actually came from those that are supposed to uphold all that is good. Societies rely on the police to serve and protect the citizenry. Prosecutors are expected to lock up the bad guys so people can sleep well at night. When corruption interferes with the systems that are put in place to protect those who need protection, the results can be devastating. Let's take a look at some of the most notable lies.

The police lied when they said Amanda was treated well during her interrogation. I believe Amanda's description of her interrogation. I believe Amanda when she says that she was hit on the back of her head. I believe Amanda when she says that she was not given food or allowed any bathroom breaks. I believe Amanda when she says she was told having an attorney would only make things worse for her. I certainly do not believe that Amanda was treated well.

Even if you choose not to believe Amanda regarding the slaps to the back of her head, the fact that she wasn't provided an attorney must certainly be looked upon as mistreatment. There is also no doubt that Amanda was kept up the entire night during questioning. If they were so accommodating to Amanda they would have had no problem turning over the audio or video recording of the interrogation. As we all know, that was never done. Are we really supposed to believe the interrogation wasn't recorded?

The prosecution lied when it misrepresented a childhood nickname given to Amanda. As discussed in chapter five, the prosecution used the media to create their fictional character Foxy Knoxy. The prosecution was well aware of the fact that this was a childhood nickname given to Amanda. The truth was not important. The goal was to destroy the character of the accused.

The postal police lied on two separate occasions. The first lies came very early on from the first police officers to arrive at the scene. The postal police testified that they showed up at the cottage twenty minutes before they actually did. The video from the camera across the street proved they arrived twenty minutes later. This lie caused major problems for Raffaele. As discussed in chapter eleven, the case was made that Raffaele called the Carabinieri after the postal police arrived. This became a major issue that was used against Raffaele in the preliminary trial deciding whether he would be held in custody.

The postal police lied again when they stated they never set foot inside Meredith's room. Michele Battistelli, one of the first police officers to arrive at the scene, denied he had entered Meredith's bedroom after the door was kicked in. His claims were refuted by two witnesses that claim to have seen Battistelli enter the room and lift up the duvet. These two witnesses hadn't any reason to lie about Battistelli's actions; they were simply telling the events of the day. Neither of them would have had any reason to think it was a problem for a police officer to check on Meredith to see if she was alive. I personally do not think I would have seen a problem with it at the time; the actions of the officer are not nearly as important as the lies he later told.

Luca Altieri said he had seen Battistelli bend down to lift a duvet that was covering Meredith's body. He was grilled about this because Battistelli had repeatedly denied entering the room. Luca was insistent about what he saw.

Luca was not the only one to see Battistelli enter the room. Marco Zaroli also claimed to have seen Battistelli enter Meredith's room. Luca's girlfriend, Paolo Grande, had not seen the officer enter but she testified that she witnessed the others talking about the officer's actions. It was during these discussions that all of the young people at the cottage became aware of the fact that Meredith's throat had been cut. If Battistelli hadn't entered the room and lifted the duvet, how would anyone have known how Meredith was killed?

An unnamed police source told Richard Owen of *The Times London* that they found receipts showing the purchase of bleach on the morning after the murder. He went with the story, though no such receipts exist. Lies were told that Amanda Knox was seen waiting at the store the morning after Meredith was murdered, waiting to buy bleach. It was widely reported that the authorities had bleach receipts proving that Amanda purchased bleach. On November 19, 2007, Richard Owen reported for the *The Times London* that police had found receipts showing purchases of bleach on the morning after the murder. The information was specific: one alleged purchase was made at 8:30 am, and a second was made at 9:15 am. No receipts were ever found. The register was investigated at the store where the alleged purchase was made. There were no sales for bleach rung up on the register.

Then, in a November 25, 2007 report, Owen quoted an "official" source as saying that the entire cottage— except for Meredith's room and the bathroom she shared with Amanda—had been "thoroughly cleaned with bleach."

It was reported that Amanda and Raffaele were caught by surprise that morning, standing on the porch of the cottage with a mop bucket and bleach when the postal police arrived.

The truth is Amanda never purchased bleach. No receipts were presented at trial. Amanda and Raffaele weren't caught by surprise. As we know, Raffaele had already called the police to report a possible break-in. The mop bucket at the cottage was investigated and no evidence was presented in regard to a mop bucket.

This story was told around the world. This lie is still being told. On December 10, 2009, Anne Coulter repeated this lie on *The O'Reilly Factor*.

There have also been reports that Raffaele purchased bleach and that receipts were found in his apartment showing proof of this purchase. Once again, this is simply false. Raffaele's apartment was thoroughly searched. Receipts were found in his apartment, but none of the receipts indicated a purchase of bleach. The police took video of the receipts that were found.

The entire media storm regarding alleged bleach purchases and clean-up efforts all started from a lie leaked by the authorities.

Giuliano Mignini lied regarding luminol tests conducted at Raffaele's apartment. Steve Moore details this lie in his article "Luminol Lies," written for Injustice in Perugia.

When Raffeale's apartment was investigated on November 13, 2007, investigators found approximately fourteen stains that glowed with luminol. None of these stains were blood, and there was no sign of any detailed clean-up effort in the apartment. Steve sums it up perfectly in his article:

> *"How can we be sure that the luminol 'hits' were not blood? Because finding blood would be damaging evidence, and Mignini would have used it. How do we know that the scene wasn't cleaned with bleach? Because of the 14 luminol 'hits', and the fact that a clean up would be damaging evidence, and Mignini would have used it."*

Two weeks after the tests were conducted Mignini filed court documents alleging that Amanda and Raffaele cleaned both the cottage and Raffaele's apartment with bleach. He knew that to be untrue. He continued to repeat this lie throughout the course of the trial.

Photos were leaked to the press showing a bathroom apparently soaked in blood. The prosecution released crime scene photos apparently showing a bloody bathroom. The public was told that Amanda returned to the apartment and took a shower in a bathroom soaked in blood.

The truth is the bathroom had been sprayed with a chemical that turns pink when it makes contact with any protein. The entire bathroom had been sprayed with this chemical. The photo that was released looked like a scene from a low-budget slasher film. The bathroom that Amanda showered in looked nothing like the photo released by the prosecutor. The photo was released with no explanation whatsoever, leaving people to wonder if it was possible that Amanda could really be that evil. This was one of many leaks by the prosecution designed to turn the public against Amanda Knox. The blood that was actually visible in the bathroom was nowhere near as apparent as the photo insinuated. There were small traces of blood on the sink and in the bidet. There was also a partial print on the bathmat made in a blood and water mixture. This print was very faint on the rug. These observations concerned Amanda, but she certainly did not shower in a blood-soaked room.

It was reported that Amanda and Raffaele used the washing machine to destroy evidence. This is another case where the police misinformed the media. In Richard Owen's November 25 report mentioned above, he says police heard the washing machine spinning to the end of its cycle when they arrived at the cottage. Other media reports repeated this claim. The stories varied from article to article. As it turned out, there was nothing incriminating at all in the washing machine. Meredith had clothes in the washer. Nothing in the washer had been worn at the time of her murder. Meredith had simply been doing laundry. At the trial, there was never any mention of the washing machine running when the postal police arrived. This was another myth that spread throughout the media—all started by another lie leaked by the authorities.

The prosecution lied on December 18, 2007 when they told the media that the book Amanda claimed to have been reading at Raffaele's apartment was instead found at the cottage. It was leaked to the media that investigators had collected the *Harry Potter* German edition book from Amanda's apartment. Amanda Knox had stated that she spent the night at Raffaele's apartment on the night of Meredith's murder. She stated that they watched the film *Amelie* and read *Harry Potter* in German. Finding this book was another blow to Amanda's alibi.

The leaked story was a complete lie. Police video clearly showed the *Harry Potter* German edition book at Raffaele's apartment as the apartment was being searched for evidence. Amanda had purchased two German language *Harry Potter* books during her trip to Germany. She took one of the books to Raffaele's. The information was leaked to further damage her reputation. This evidence was never presented at trial, bearing out the fact that it was yet another fabrication. This lie was leaked on Tuesday, December 18, 2007, shortly before a final hearing was to take place before the Italian Supreme Court to decide if Amanda and Raffaele would remain in custody until their trial.

Manuela Comodi lied in court about the call made "before anything happened." When assistant prosecutor Manuela Comodi questioned Amanda, she accused Amanda of calling her mother at noon—before anything had happened. The truth is Amanda did not make that call until 12:47 pm. At that point, Amanda had already spoken to Raffaele about her concerns. In fact, this call was made after Amanda and Raffaele had discovered the broken window. Amanda had already called Filomena four times before she made the call to her mother. Both Raffaele and Filomena had expressed their concerns to Amanda, leading her to become even more concerned about the situation. Calling her mother was a very normal reaction for a young woman confronted with a stressful situation in a foreign country.

The prosecution's expert, Dr. Lorenzo Rinaldi, lied about the size of Guede's foot to create the false impression that it was too big to have made the print on the bathmat. As discussed in chapter ten, Rinaldi stated the width of Rudy's foot was 66.7 mm, when in reality his foot was 55.2 mm. Rinaldi's entire presentation was useless because he started with an incorrect measurement of Rudy's foot. Rudy's foot was not too big to have made the print on the bathmat. I do not believe this was simply negligence on Rinaldi's part; I believe this to be an outright lie. How could this expert use the wrong measurement for the floor tile when analyzing the luminol stains and also make this egregious error when analyzing the stain left on the bathmat?

Stefanoni lied about performing a second blood test on the luminol footprints, saying that no such test was performed. When evidence collection was completed on December 18, investigators sprayed the floor with luminol. Stefanoni claimed in court that the stains detected with luminol were never tested for blood; however, in July 2009, when pressured by the defense, Stefanoni released information originally withheld. Stefanoni's notes confirmed the stains were tested with tetramethylbenzidine, which is extremely sensitive for blood. All of the stains detected with luminol tested negative for blood. Patrizia Stefanoni and Manuela Comodi both chose to ignore the test results during the trial.

Stefanoni lied again when she testified that she changed gloves every time she handled a new sample. Raffaele's defense clearly showed in court that Stefanoni lied about her gloves. This information was not given proper weight at trial. The fact that she lied not only puts her credibility into question, it also shows that Stefanoni felt that her negligence was significant enough to hide it with a lie. If she felt it had no bearing on the reliability of the evidence, she certainly wouldn't have risked her reputation by lying. As you have already read in the contamination chapter, nothing is more important than changing gloves during evidence collection. Stefanoni's negligence at the scene of the crime heavily compromised

the evidence. Lying in court heavily damaged her
reputation.

**Judge Massei lied when he stated the text message
from Patrick to Amanda on the evening of November
1 was handled by a cell tower that does not cover
Raffaele's apartment.** Massei did this to insinuate that
Amanda was not at Raffaele's the entire night, therefore
making her a liar. Yet the cell tower in question (Via
dell'Aquila 5-Torre dell'Acquedotto sector 3) did cover
Raffaele's apartment, and Massei knew it.

The following day, Amanda made three phone calls
from Raffaele's apartment and also received a call from
Filomena. Massei details all four of these calls in the
Motivation report. When Amanda returned to Raffaele's
on the morning of November 2, she called Filomena and
both of Meredith's cell phones. She then received a return
call from Filomena.

All four of these calls were handled by the same cell
tower that handled the text message from Patrick. Massei
knew the cell tower serviced Raffaele's apartment. Did
Massei think that no one would notice that he completely
contradicted himself in the motivation? Unlike Massei,
Amanda was being completely honest when she said she
was at Raffaele's apartment when she received the text
from Patrick.

**The prosecution lied when they stated that Amanda
and Raffaele repeatedly lied.** The truth is that a majority

of their accusations are based on information collected during interrogation. Amanda and Raffaele didn't repeatedly change their alibis. Their account of events changed only once, and this occurred during interrogation. Amanda stated just hours after the interrogation ended that the signed statements were not the truth. Raffaele attempted to explain to Judge Claudia Matteini during a preliminary trial that his statements came at a time of extreme stress.

So where are all of these additional lies? Where are the multiple alibis? Raffaele only spoke to the police on two occasions. He was questioned on November 2, when everyone was ordered to the station from the cottage, and then again on November 5. During the first round of questioning, Raffaele told the truth. He said that he and Amanda spent the evening together. Amanda was questioned repeatedly. Her account of the events was always the same. Amanda repeatedly told the truth. Her account of the events changed only once.

Amanda and Raffaele had their phone conversations recorded from the very beginning. They both had no idea they were being recorded. There wasn't one single incriminating statement made during those conversations. Not one. This is a very significant observation. Two young people made dozens of calls during a time of extreme stress. Not once did either of them say anything that would substantiate their guilt. Why? Because Amanda and Raffaele are innocent.

So how were these accusations of repeated lies justified? Amanda and Raffaele's normal activities were exaggerated and the truth was manipulated to fabricate circumstances that never occurred. This is not just my opinion. This has been repeatedly proven throughout this case. The prosecution's claim that Amanda lied about what time she ate dinner on the night of the murder is a perfect example of this.

After repeated questioning regarding the events of November 1, 2007, Amanda gave two different times for when she thought she had eaten dinner. The prosecution accused Amanda of lying— pushing the dinner to a later time in an attempt to create an alibi.

However, Amanda has always stated she did not remember exactly what time she and Raffaele had dinner. Amanda repeatedly stated during interrogation the night of November 6, 2007 that she found it very difficult to remember the exact hours of dinner and the movie on November 1, 2007. During her June 12, 2009 testimony, Amanda stated:

"We talked, we had dinner, and we had not left the apartment. I had not looked at the clock. I am not able to tell exactly what time I did everything."

Amanda also stated that she did not remember the exact order of the evening's events. It is a very arbitrary assumption that Amanda postponed the time of dinner based upon her statement that she did not know the exact timeline of her activities.

Amanda did the best she could to recount the events of the evening and was very truthful in doing so. If any of us were grilled about the exact details of any given day, it would be completely normal if we were to get a detail or two wrong. As we live our lives, we do not record every single detail of our day into memory. We do not assume that we will be quizzed on our daily events at a later time. There was nothing incriminating about Amanda's failure to remember exactly what time she ate dinner.

As you can see, there were many lies told throughout the course of this case, but Amanda and Raffaele weren't the ones telling them.

I will conclude this chapter with one of the most disturbing acts of misconduct that I've observed. The slander charges that have been leveled against Amanda Knox and her parents show an extreme abuse of power. These charges are disturbing because they attempt to prevent the accused from defending her innocence.

In any civilized society, the accused deserves the right to face their accuser and defend their innocence. Amanda Knox took the stand and testified in her own defense. For doing so, she was slapped with a slander charge that can add six years to her sentence. This is absolutely preposterous.

I would feel the same way even if I felt that Amanda was guilty. The conviction is the punishment. The prosecution should not have the power to punish the accused by tacking years onto their sentence for speaking in defense of their own innocence.

Amanda has been charged with slandering the police department for stating that she was repeatedly hit on the back of the head during her interrogation. Some will say that this lawsuit comes from the police department and not the prosecution. This is complete nonsense. Mignini has been running the show from the beginning and there is no doubt that he influenced the police to file this lawsuit.

Amanda has been accused of not being able to identify her attacker. This insinuation is completely false. Here is an excerpt from an interrogation conducted by Mignini.

Amanda: Well, there were lots and lots of people who were asking me questions, but the person who had started talking with me was a policewoman with long hair, chestnut brown hair, but I don't know her. Then in the circle of people who were around me, certain people asked me questions, for example there was a man who was holding my telephone, and who was literally shoving the telephone into my face, shouting "Look at this telephone! Who is this? Who did you want to meet?" Then there were others, for instance this woman who was leading, was the same person who at one point was standing behind me, because they kept moving, they were really surrounding me and on top of me. I was sitting on a chair, then the interpreter was also sitting on a chair, and everyone else was standing around me, so I didn't see who gave me the first blow because it was someone behind me, but then I turned around and saw that woman, and she gave me another blow to the head.

Mignini: This was the same woman with the long hair?

Amanda: Yes, the same one.

We all know the recording of the interrogation has never been released. So the slander trial will essentially be Amanda's word against the police. This does not really seem fair, does it? Well, it gets worse. Remember the judge that chastised Amanda for not showing remorse for a crime she did not commit? That's right, Mignini's good friend Judge Claudia Matteini. Well, Judge Matteini has now been assigned to Amanda's slander trial.

The defense requested another judge, of course, but their request was denied. Can someone please tell me how this is possible? Why on earth has this not caused more outrage?

The fact that Amanda's parents were also charged with slander should be a huge red flag for all of Italy. This is an obvious attempt to intimidate all involved and to put fear into the minds of anyone who disagrees with the authorities.

Amanda's parents face slander charges over comments they made in a 2008 interview to a British newspaper. Here are the quotes made during an interview with *The Times London* that brought the slander charges:

> *"Amanda was abused physically and verbally. She told us she was hit in the back of the head by a police officer with an open hand, at least twice."*

> *"The police told her, 'If you ask for a lawyer, things will get worse for you' and 'If you don't give us some explanation for what happened, you're going to go to jail for a very long time.'"*

Amanda's parents are being charged with a crime in Italy for making those statements to a British newspaper. I do not know if there could possibly be a better example of an inexcusable abuse of power.

We know the prosecution committed many acts of misconduct. This behavior is very dangerous and this information should be disturbing to anyone who reads it. This conduct should be most alarming to Italians. These actions threaten their freedom. Italians need to stand up against this misconduct and refuse to be silent until this injustice is corrected. There is much to be learned from cases like these. If the problems are addressed and proper action is taken against all involved, tragedies like this can be prevented in the future.

Italian Justice

I am certainly no expert when it comes to Italian law, but certain fundamental values are expected to be present in any democracy. I am often told that I just don't understand Italian law, as if that is supposed to somehow convince me that an injustice has not occurred. Of course, for the most part, these statements are true. I still have much to learn about Italian law, but facts are facts, and the evidence in this case would have looked the same in a U.S. court as it did in an Italian court. It was not the location of the courtroom that caused the problem. The main cause of this injustice was not the system of law that was in place but rather the individuals that were assigned to uphold those laws. Keep in mind; this is the same justice system that also convicted Giuliano Mignini.

You don't need to be an expert in Italian law to see that an injustice occurred in this case. This injustice was committed by a small group of individuals that abused their power to protect their own interests. The focus should be on those individuals. No system of law is perfect. Unfortunately, corrupt individuals exist in every system. Lead investigator Edgardo Giobbi and lead prosecutor Giuliano Mignini are the two people that we need to focus on when it comes to placing blame for this injustice. There's plenty of blame to go around, but Mignini and Giobbi share the brunt of it.

The case was solved in record time—long before any evidence had been collected. When the actual truth came to light and Rudy Guede was arrested, the initial mistake could have been corrected, but fragile reputations were on the line. Careers would be made on this case; personal interest outweighed the truth.

I don't honestly think that the entire police force in Perugia was part of a big conspiracy against Amanda and Raffaele. The investigators believed they were doing the right thing because they were told by the higher-ups that Amanda and Raffaele were guilty. Believing that they were guilty allowed them to justify bending the rules to bring the desired results. This is often the case when corruption occurs at a high level of authority. Giuliano

Mignini quickly took charge. He told the police what to look for. He told them what evidence to analyze and what evidence to disregard. There is no doubt that he influenced Perugia's Police Chief, Arturo De Felice, to declare "case closed." This is an awful lot of power to hand over to a corrupt man like Mignini.

Italy does not deserve a free pass when it comes to placing blame. No country that has an injustice occur in their system of law ever does. Looking at this trial from a distance, there were certain aspects of Italian law that concerned me. I am sure Italians could draw up a long list of U.S. laws that concern them as well. I am certainly not making the claim that United States law is perfect by any means. I just want to point out some procedural issues I have with the way this trial in particular was conducted in Italy:

- Giuliano Mignini should not have been permitted to prosecute this case. He was on trial for abuse of office while he was prosecuting Amanda and Raffaele's trial. A prosecutor that is on trial for abuse of office should not be prosecuting cases until the outcome of their trial is complete. As we know, Mignini was later found guilty and, as of this writing, is awaiting appeal. Italian law permits him to continue to prosecute even after his conviction. He will hold onto his power until his conviction is confirmed on appeal. I understand this is the same appeals process that will give Amanda and Raffaele another chance to defend their innocence. I personally feel that a convicted prosecutor should at least be given a different role until his appeals are exhausted. I look at it in the same regard as a police officer being given a desk job if they are currently being investigated for misconduct.

- A preliminary court hearing was held on November 8, 2007, in the courtroom of Judge Claudia Matteini to decide if the suspects would be held in jail for up to a year while further investigation was conducted. I find this aspect of Italian law to be disturbing. The defense attorneys met with their clients for the first time at that hearing. There was absolutely no way to prepare any type of counter argument. In these preliminary hearings, if the judge sides with the prosecutor, the suspects sit in prison for a year waiting for the chance to defend their innocence.

- The jury was not sequestered. Italy does not have jurors; they actually use the term "lay judges." I have chosen to use the American equivalent in this case to avoid confusion. The jurors associated with the lawyers when they went out to lunch at restaurants during the trial. During court recess, jurors had lunch and coffee at the same cafes as the lawyers and journalists did. Jurors were allowed to discuss the case and follow all the press coverage. I understand that trials in Italy can go for long periods of time which can make sequestering a jury impossible in many cases. Therefore a more stringent guideline ought to be put in place to keep jurors from associating with others involved in the trial or from reading news reports.

- The civil trial ran at the same time as the murder trial. The interrogation of Amanda Knox was ruled inadmissible in the murder trial by the Italian Supreme Court. The civil trial was conducted at the same time as the murder trial, so the jury heard the results of the illegal interrogation anyway. The prosecution was able to ignore the Supreme Court ruling by presenting the information to the exact same jury during the civil trial. I believe that running the civil trial during the murder trial conveys a presumption of guilt. Amanda and Raffaele were being sued for money before they were given a chance to defend their innocence.

The details I mentioned above are observations I made while watching this trial unfold. One aspect of Italian law that I failed to notice until I became more involved with this case is the fact that court documents are not readily available to the public. When I really began to do serious research, the fact that Italian courts lacked transparency became glaringly evident to me. This is an important issue that has received little attention throughout the course of this trial. Joseph Bishop passionately discusses this topic below. I have great respect for Joseph and I truly admire his dedication to this cause. He has worked tirelessly to debunk the vile garbage that infests comment boards online as well as researched extensively to expose the injustice that has occurred. Joseph wrote an excellent article discussing Italy's lack of transparency regarding trial documents for Injustice in Perugia:

The Trial of Amanda Knox and Public Access to Trial Documents by Joseph Bishop

The public's right to access court documents and other important public records is a fundamental principal of any democracy. The recent trial in Perugia, Italy, of American exchange student Amanda Knox for the murder of her British housemate, Meredith Kercher, has generated international controversy over Ms. Knox's guilty verdict. The important public debate about the case has been hampered by an almost complete lack of public access to the trial record.

Amanda Knox and Raffaele Sollecito were found guilty of Ms. Kercher's murder on December 4, 2009. With the exception of a single judicial opinion in the case, not one document from the Knox trial has ever been published to the Internet where those with an interest in the case can see for themselves if justice was done. This is in sharp contrast to the United States and other Western democracies where non-sealed documents are often available online in pdf format and always available from the courthouse.

The Knox trial was fraught with controversy and a vast Internet blog debate has raged on for years. It is important to examine where the public's information has come from in the case.

Trial sessions were for the most part open to the public. Some of Amanda Knox's testimony was broadcast to video screens outside the courtroom where it was recorded and later distributed on the Internet. More often online newspaper or magazine articles would report what their reporters could remember from the daily court session.

An important third source of information was selected documents released by law enforcement officials to favored members of the press. These have included autopsy photos of the victim that never should have been in the public domain and other information that was patently false. Since jury members were not prohibited from viewing media reporting on the case, the release of such information took on extra importance. Other non-sensitive materials, such as crime scene video, have been circulated behind the scenes to interested parties but always carry a requirement that the information may not be published.

Observers of the case have emphasized that significant information released prior to trial was false. Seattle area Superior Court Judge Michael Heavey stated, "What I saw was a tremendous amount of not only leaks going to the press which demonized Amanda Knox, but the leaks were false." Another close observer of the case, CBS News correspondent Peter Van Sant, went on to say, "They [the jury] were subject to this avalanche of negative tabloid reporting, much of which were complete lies."

In the United States, courts have historically provided copies of documents, made available at the courthouse for about a dollar a page. Starting in 2001, Federal Courts have operated the PACER (Public Access to Courts Electronic Records) system available at www.pacer.gov. Non-sealed documents are available for immediate download to anyone in the world for $0.08 per page in pdf format. State Courts have generally been slow to adopt such new technology. In New York, the SCROLL (Supreme Court Records On-Line Library) provides access similar to the PACER system but is free.

There are of course many legitimate reasons for denying public access to certain court records and the law here can be complicated. Such documents are sealed and not available to the public. Obvious examples include material that might compromise the dignity of the victim or the privacy of minors, or that which would put witnesses in jeopardy.

The case of Carlo Parlanti illustrates the difference between the Italian and United States systems. Mr. Parlanti is an Italian man currently in jail in California for sexual assault who many Italians believe is innocent. Numerous court documents

chosen by the defense are available at
www.carloparlanti.com.

Transparency of judicial proceedings is an
important part of any democracy. The Italian legal
process is not transparent. *

Joseph's words could not be more true. I think this is a
very important issue that, unfortunately, will most likely
not be addressed anytime soon.

Of course, I also have a list of issues that I disagree
with when it comes to the United States justice system.
But that list is for another book. The injustice committed
against Amanda and Raffaele occurred in Italy, so the
Italian system of justice will remain our focus for now.

How do Italians feel about their current justice system?

Foreignpolicy.com reports that many Italians are angered
by the unreliability of their court system. According to a
November 2009 poll by Euromedia research group, only
sixteen percent of Italians fully trust the current justice
system in Italy. Just two years ago, the figure was twenty-
eight percent. Italian civil rights groups are intense in
their criticism of what they view as kangaroo courts.

Roberto Malini, president of EveryOne, a
nongovernmental organization that defends ethnic
minorities in jail, states that inquiries are conducted
without any reliable methods. Roberto also states that

tests take place solely in the laboratories of the state police. There is no independent lab, and independent observers do not have access to police work.

A conservative newspaper in Italy published an interview with Marco Morin, a Venice-based firearms expert. Marco said that he didn't want to work in Italian courts.

"In the United States, federal judges must study a 637-page manual in order to be able to evaluate forensic evidence. Here, they accept everything without questioning, as long as it comes from the institutional laboratory."

Judge Francesco Cananzi, a representative of the national council of magistrates, said, *"Here in Italy trials take place on TV, rather than in court."*

The European Court of Justice routinely sanctions Italy due to its drawn-out legal processes. The current system runs very slowly. A criminal trial can take five to six years. Italy's system is severely backlogged. Official figures show that there are over 3.5 million criminal cases and 5.5 million civil cases waiting to see a courtroom. Many innocent people spend years sitting in prison simply waiting for the system to eventually acquit them.

I believe serious reform is needed with regard to how trials operate in Italy. This is my opinion, of course, but there must be a solution to the severe backlog of cases that currently plague Italian courts. Preliminary judges are overwhelmed and cannot possibly have the time to properly address each case before making a decision. It would be reasonable to say that their workload would persuade them to move the cases along quickly with the belief that everything will be worked out at the criminal trial. The current system leads to many people being held in prison for long periods of time.

Trials in Italy have similarities to United States trials, but there are some stark differences. This trial has highlighted several procedural differences between Italy and the U.S. Prosecutors are powerful figures in Italy. They are connected to the judiciary but are not elected or appointed officials. Prosecutors in Italy lead the entire investigation which means they have a much different role than a prosecutor in the U.S. Douglas Preston, who knows from personal experience how the system works, had this to say:

> *"Prosecutors are firmly in charge. They tell the police what to look for, where to go, what evidence to analyze, what evidence not to analyze. In America, the police work independently and are specifically trained in evidence gathering and criminal investigation. In Italy, the police must do what the prosecutor tells them. As a result, many criminal investigations in Italy are botched by prosecutors who are judges, trained in the law, who have no background in criminal investigation, police work, or forensic science."*

Italian jury trials look quite different than U.S. jury trials. When it comes to serious crimes such as murder, eight judges hear the case: two professional judges and six lay judges. The two professional judges guide the jury as it sorts through the facts of the case. One of the professional judges acts as the lead judge and runs the court proceedings. The judge that runs the trial in court also has a vote on the guilt or innocence of the accused. This judge is also the leader, which naturally influences the opinion of the other judges. The ruling only needs to be a simple majority. You can be sentenced to life in prison on a 5–3 vote.

Keep in mind; the six lay judges are citizens of the town that are chosen at random with no screening by the prosecution or the defense. From my perspective, it certainly appears that the six lay judges have far less control over the outcome of the trial than jurors in the U.S. Far more power is given to the judge in Italian courts.

The appeals process
The defendants and the prosecutor can appeal the judgment before the court of appeals. In this case, the prosecution is appealing the convictions. Mignini wants the sentences increased to life in prison. This means there is a possibility that sentences could be increased on appeal.

If the first appeal does not correct this injustice, the judgment can be appealed again before the Italian Supreme Court. The high court does not rule on the evidence but rather on the interpretation or application of the law. The high court has the responsibility of making sure the lower court followed proper legal procedure.

The first appeal will be heard at the Corte d'Assise d'Appello (court of appeals). As in the first trial, eight judges will hear the case: two professional judges and six lay judges. The lay judges must meet higher standards of education than the lay judges in the first trial.

Italy has a justice system that relies heavily on the appeals system. You are given two chances to appeal your ruling. Fifty percent of rulings are overturned or adjusted on appeal. The Italian Justice System does not consider you guilty until your appeals are completed.

This case is one that should be studied long after the appeals are exhausted and the case is finalized. Nothing can bring back lost years for Amanda and Raffaele; but with any luck, lessons will be learned that will help eliminate wrongful convictions in the future.

Rudy Guede

If it wasn't you, then who was it? This is a question that begs an answer any time the accused proclaim their innocence. This is a major hurdle for many that have faced wrongful convictions. Of course, I completely disagree with the idea that the wrongfully accused should be held responsible for investigating and finding the actual perpetrator. Those storylines should be left for Hollywood; but unfortunately, when faced with a wrongful conviction, the question *If not you, then who?* usually remains on the minds of your accusers.

In this case, the person that committed this brutal murder is already in prison. This is what makes this case so absurd. Rudy Guede murdered Meredith Kercher. The evidence is clear. Unlike many wrongful conviction cases, once Amanda and Raffaele are exonerated there will be no mystery left to unravel.

How can I say with complete certainty that I believe Rudy Guede attacked and murdered Meredith Kercher? Unlike Amanda and Raffaele, Rudy was arrested after analysis of the evidence at the crime scene. The evidence points right to him—no one else, just him. There was no rush to judgment when it came to the arrest of Rudy Guede. Investigators found a hand print on the bed at the crime scene. The fingerprints led them to their suspect. Rudy knew he was guilty and had already fled to Germany. Thankfully, he was stopped in Germany trying to board a train without a ticket and was immediately extradited back to Italy.

The evidence against Rudy was overwhelming. Rudy admitted he was in Meredith's room at the time of the attack. His DNA along with Meredith's blood was found on Meredith's purse. His shoeprints, set in Meredith's blood, were found in the bedroom and in the hallway leading right out the front door. His hand prints, also in Meredith's blood, were found on a pillowcase underneath her body. Most importantly, Rudy's DNA was found *inside* Meredith's body. This evidence is irrefutable.

The story Rudy told to police was absurd. Rudy claimed he met Meredith at a bar and they both went back to Meredith's residence. He claimed that he and Meredith were "fooling around" in her room when he had the sudden urge to use the bathroom. While he was in the bathroom listening to his iPod, someone entered the cottage and attacked Meredith. Rudy claimed that he came out of the bathroom and confronted the attacker, who managed to break free and escape yelling:

"A black man found is a black man condemned."

Rudy said he tried to help Meredith by retrieving towels from the bathroom in an attempt stop her bleeding. He claimed that he left in a panic because he was convinced that the color of his skin would be enough to attract the attention of the Italian police. He was so panicked, apparently, that he was later seen at a nightclub—just a few hours after the murder—dancing the night away as if nothing had happened.

His story would change repeatedly as more news was made available to him. When he was in Germany, he saw how the story was unfolding and observed the media's focus on Amanda Knox. During a police-monitored phone call Rudy explicitly stated that Amanda was not present when the murder took place. He made no mention of Amanda and Raffaele in his initial story. He even went out of his way to tell an acquaintance on the phone that the media had it wrong, informing this person that Amanda was not there.

Over time, Rudy's story would change. It was apparent that he felt the need to implicate Amanda and Raffaele to try to save himself. Rudy first changed his story to say that the originally unnamed intruder he confronted was actually Raffaele. Then he later added Amanda into the equation, saying that he saw her standing off in the distance.

Rudy Guede was a small-time drug dealer and burglar who was well known by the police. At the time of Meredith's murder, he was desperate for money and was being threatened with eviction. He knew rents were coming due in Perugia and that the time would be right to find cash available in student apartments. His plans to burglarize the cottage were altered when Meredith arrived home for the evening.

Leading up to the night of the murder, Rudy had already committed a series of crimes. In an article in the British newspaper *The Daily Express*, Bob Graham reported that Rudy committed an entire series of crimes in a very short time frame:

> *"It reveals the third person convicted of killing British student Meredith Kercher had committed six serious crimes over 33 days before the killing. But robberies carried out by small-time drug dealer Rudy Guede were ignored by Italian authorities, raising suspicions that he was a police informer."*

Why were all of these crimes overlooked by the police? Why was Rudy repeatedly brought into custody and then released?

Just six days before the murder, Rudy broke into a nursery school. The owner of a Milan nursery school testified in court that Rudy Guede had broken into her school and had stolen a big kitchen knife. The nursery school's owner, Maria Del Prato, testified that she had stopped by the school on Saturday, October 27, and came upon Rudy in her office.

> *"I asked him who he was and he replied perfectly calmly, even though I had caught him red-handed, that he was a kid from Perugia who had arrived the night before and had nowhere to sleep."*

Del Prato doubted his story and said she believed Rudy was looking for something to steal. Some money was missing, and Del Prato noticed Rudy had a laptop. When police arrived at the school, they searched Rudy's backpack and found a large knife with a 16-inch blade that had been taken from the school kitchen.

Rudy was later booked at a Milan police station and accused of theft, receiving stolen goods, and in possession of a weapon. He was fingerprinted and released. It was this arrest that put his fingerprints on file, allowing the police to later identify him in Meredith's murder.

As it turns out, the laptop that Del Prato observed in Rudy's possession was stolen. Rudy broke into a law office on the night of October 13, 2007. To gain access to the law office, Rudy threw a large rock through a second story window and climbed up using a metal grate on a door below the window.

There are also reports that Rudy broke into the home of Cristian Tramontano. When Rudy was confronted by Tramontano, he pulled out a knife and threatened him with it. The confrontation ended when Rudy ran away. On four occasions, Tramontano went to the police station to report the break-in, identify Rudy as the culprit, and detail how Rudy threatened him with a knife. On each occasion, Tramontano says he was ignored and the police refused to listen to him. How could the police ignore a man telling them he was threatened by an armed intruder in his own home?

What is even more disturbing is that there appears to be a cover up of other crimes committed by Rudy as well. We do not have police reports from all of Rudy's criminal activity. Graham reported that Rudy committed six crimes in the month leading up to the murder, yet we have no information from the authorities detailing these crimes. Why is this information being withheld? Was Rudy an informant? Were police protecting him, or was this just a case of poor police work? It would be expected that an informant would be protected so he could keep feeding information to the authorities. A burglary or two that goes unsolved in order to keep an informant out on the streets may have appeared worth the risk of protecting him. But in this case, it went horribly wrong. If Rudy was an informant and he was protected, the police would have had good reason to try and cover it up.

We know what Rudy did: the evidence is clear. We know he was a small-time burglar that was repeatedly given free passes to try again until, inevitably, a horrific tragedy occurred.

Unfortunately many questions still remain about the actions of the authorities. Whether or not Rudy was an informant is purely speculation at this point. There is no explanation for how the authorities acted, but the theory that he was an informant would certainly help explain it. The only way we'll ever get to the truth is if someone in the police force comes forward and speaks out. It is imperative that this information be brought to light so the truth can finally be heard.

No matter what the reason preventing it, one thing is very clear: Rudy should have been in custody on the night of Meredith's murder. Even Giuliano Mignini said Rudy should have been in jail at the time of the murder. If the prior crimes of Rudy Guede were handled properly by the Perugian authorities, Meredith Kercher would still be alive today.

The actions of the authorities not only failed to protect Meredith, they also opened the door for three innocent people to be arrested for her murder. If the crime scene were properly examined early on, the investigation would have gone much differently. The scene should have been viewed as a burglary gone horribly wrong. From looking at the evidence presented at the cottage, it was obvious a break-in occurred. If investigators had researched similar crimes that had recently happened in Perugia, Rudy would have been suspected within the first 24 hours. He would have been brought in for questioning long before he had a chance to flee the country.

Investigators would have seen the fresh wounds on his hands. He would have still been in possession of the shoes that he wore the night of the murder. Shoeprints and fingerprints would have matched the crime scene. This evidence alone would have been more than enough, yet there is no telling what else would have been discovered if Rudy had been investigated immediately.

If this evidence was brought to light in the first 24 hours, this tragedy would not have been compounded. Additional victims wouldn't have been created. There wouldn't have been time for Mignini's mind to concoct his fantasy. There wouldn't have been a press conference declaring "case closed."

When you look at how this case was handled, it becomes very clear why the authorities tried so hard to cover it up. It is time for the truth; not only to release those who are innocent, but also to learn from this tragedy so that it won't happen again in the future.

The court had ample opportunity to correct this injustice but chose to look the other way. The court chose to ignore Rudy's criminal past. When you think about it, they really had no choice. If they had acknowledged Rudy's past, they would have had to take another look at the break-in. We all know how important the accusation of staging has been to this entire case. If the break-in was not staged, the entire case against Amanda and Raffaele would fall apart. What else could the court do? Rudy's past had to be ignored in order to achieve the desired verdict.

In the preface of this book, I wrote the following: Even if this injustice is corrected and both Amanda and Raffaele are fully exonerated, there will be no winners in this case. Unfortunately, the damage has already been done. Everyone loses.

Unfortunately I was not entirely correct when I wrote that statement. When it is all said and done, as disgusted as I am to say it, the only winner in this case will be Rudy Guede. Rudy is a young man still, and—due to the complete mishandling of this case—he has many years of freedom in his future.

Common Sense

Investigators were well aware of the fact that there was no evidence in the murder room to suggest that Amanda and Raffaele were present at the time of the murder. They were also aware of the fact that Giuliano Mignini was telling them the two were involved. With this in mind, they made a desperate attempt to procure incriminating evidence to satisfy Mignini's request.

We have already discussed the shoe prints that investigators attempted to attribute to Amanda and Raffaele early on. Of course, both of those shoe prints belonged to Rudy Guede. With absolutely nothing to work with, investigators tried to make the shoe prints work in their favor and failed miserably.

If you have listened to news reports regarding this case then you have undoubtedly heard one of Amanda's attorneys, Theodore Simon, detailing the lack of evidence. You may begin to wonder why you keep hearing the same information over and over again on the news. The reason is simple. The truth will be repeated over and over again until this injustice is corrected.

There was absolutely no credible evidence in the murder room that could be attributed to Amanda and Raffaele. Not one fingerprint, palm print, shoe print, or footprint; no hair, no saliva, no bodily fluid of any kind, and no DNA. All of the evidence collected in the murder room pointed to one man: Rudy Guede.

And yet, the court looked past the absence of evidence and suggested the bra clasp proved Amanda and Raffaele were involved. We know the clasp has absolutely no credibility. So how could Amanda and Raffaele have been involved in the murder if there was no evidence of their presence in the murder room?

Maybe Amanda and Raffaele were blessed with the gift of flight. After all, this is the only way they could have participated in Meredith's murder. Considering everything else the prosecution managed to pull off in the courtroom, maybe they should have made this suggestion to the jury. Maybe Mignini could have presented an animated movie showing Amanda and Raffaele flying around the room. I wish I were only being comical; Mignini actually used an animated film during his closing argument. The court was presented with an extremely unprofessional and highly offensive animated movie depicting Amanda, Raffaele, and Rudy attacking Meredith.

The defense could have easily created an animated movie featuring Rudy as the killer. Is that how cases should be tried? Whoever creates the best animated short film wins. What nonsense. At some point we need to employ some common sense. We all know Amanda and Raffaele cannot fly. Therefore, common sense tells us they were not present at the time of the murder. The truth was clear from very early on but was completely ignored.

The Italian courts have a post-trial obligation that is not seen in the United States. The court is required to write a report called a motivation explaining the reasoning that led to their conclusions. In this case, the court's motivation document was released to the public on March 4, 2010. This report is also referred to as the Massei report because Judge Massei was its primary author. This report contains over 400 pages of speculation, going to great lengths to explain away any doubt regarding the convictions of Amanda Knox and Raffaele Sollecito. No one can argue that the report is short on words, but one thing it most certainly lacks is common sense.

Having the lead judge in an Italian jury trial write the motivation report may seem like a good idea at first, but I believe it reveals some very telling information about Italian jury trials. To me, it shows just how much influence the lead judge actually has. Keep in mind, this judge guides and advises the jury throughout the trial. Does Italy really have jury trials or are they actually controlled by the judges? Did the jurors feel obligated to go along with the wishes of their leader? One juror spoke out after the trial:

> *"It was hard to envision Knox doing this," she said. "But it is possible. We can all drink too much, then get in a car and drive."*

This juror didn't seem very convinced to me. It sounds like she went along because she was told Amanda was guilty, not because she necessarily saw convincing evidence. It seems more like, *"Well, this is what they are telling me so I guess it's possible."* Is this really the attitude we hope to see from a juror who just condemned two people to a quarter century behind bars?

The court's decisions in the motivation report further arouse questions of whether the jury is more or less controlled by the court. After listening to eleven months of testimony from the prosecution, the court flat out rejected the prosecution's entire theory of the crime and decided to create one of its own. I find this astonishing.

How could the court simply disregard the prosecution's arguments and still arrive at a guilty verdict? How did the six jurors who weren't judges feel about this? Were they involved in that decision to reject the prosecution's theory, or was this an example of how Massei guided them to believe what he wanted them to believe?

The court dismissed the prosecution's theory that Meredith was murdered because Amanda resented her, and there is no mention in the document of a sex game gone wrong. The court also makes no mention of the three alleged attackers meeting up at any time prior to the attack as the prosecution suggested. The court believes that Rudy Guede was the instigator and Amanda and Raffaele joined in. In order for this theory to work, common sense must be thrown out the window.

As discussed, Amanda and Raffaele had been dating for just under a week at the time of the murder. During that time, Amanda had been sleeping at Raffaele's so the two could be alone.

The court suggested that Amanda and Raffaele decided to change their routine on the night of the murder. Instead of enjoying the complete privacy of Raffaele's apartment, the court believes that they went to the cottage to be intimate in Amanda's room. Why would Amanda and Raffaele leave the privacy of Raffaele's apartment to go the cottage where Amanda's roommate would be home? Meredith hadn't told anyone she planned to be away. Amanda would have assumed she'd be at home. To suggest that Amanda and Raffaele would prefer the cottage over Raffaele's apartment makes little sense.

The court's theory of the attack is mind-boggling. The court suggested that Amanda and Raffaele were being intimate in Amanda's room when they heard Meredith getting attacked. At that time, they both went to Meredith's room and witnessed the attack in progress. Influenced by smoking marijuana along with Raffaele's memories of violent comic books, they decided to join in on the attack. I guess the court assumed that at that time, Amanda ran to her bag to fetch Raffaele's kitchen knife they claimed she had been carrying around for protection.

What? This theory is not just ridiculous, this theory is insane. Why would Amanda decide to help a virtual stranger attack and murder her friend? Why would Raffaele just go along with that? How would they have known that Rudy would not attack them? Are we really supposed to believe they both entered the room and saw the attack in progress, and not only had absolutely no fear of the attacker but also decided to assist in the attack?

Common sense, based on the facts provided, tells us that Amanda and Raffaele were not at the cottage on the night of the murder. And we know, as discussed in chapter seven, that Amanda was not carrying around Raffaele's kitchen knife for self-defense. The knife was safe and sound in his kitchen drawer on the night of the murder. So if the court had it all wrong, then what really happened?

The truth is clear to anyone willing to see it. Rudy Guede broke Filomena's window with a large rock, climbed up to the window using the security bars on the lower-level window, released the latch, and climbed in. After entering the cottage, Rudy needed to use the bathroom. His plans to burglarize the cottage were altered when Meredith arrived home for the evening. Meredith's arrival most likely surprised Rudy. In his haste, he neglected to flush the toilet as he made his way to Meredith's room. Rudy surprised Meredith in her room, where he fatally stabbed and sexually assaulted her.

Rudy then went into the bathroom, where he cleaned up—leaving the shoe print on the bathmat. He returned to Meredith's room and covered her body with the duvet from the bed. He then sat down on the bed and went through Meredith's things, placing the knife at his side and leaving the imprint on the sheet. A receipt found on top of the duvet covering Meredith shows that the purse had been ransacked after Meredith was covered. Rudy took Meredith's money, credit cards, phones, and keys and left the cottage, locking Meredith's door on the way out. His shoe prints, set in Meredith's blood, could be seen going out the front door.

This was a horrible murder but it was not a complicated one. The court would like us to believe that their scenario is the most logical and that any contradictory theory would have to be based on some crazy conspiracy. This is far from the truth.

Unfortunately, cases where a male attacks a female are very common. It is an extraordinary circumstance where a group sex game goes so horribly wrong that it leads to murder.

The blood evidence on the floor doesn't show signs of a group attack. The bloodstain patterns are consistent with a single attacker. Dr. Lalli, the coroner that performed the autopsy, was unable to say that there was definitively more than one attacker. Dr. Bacci, a medical examiner testifying for the prosecution, reached the same conclusion:

> *"The biological data cannot tell us if it was one or more persons who killed Meredith."*

Dr. Liviero, a police doctor testifying for the prosecution, stated:

> *"A single attacker could have done it."*

Dr. Torre, testifying for the defense, suggested only one attacker:

> *"There was a scuffle first then stabbing, that could have been from one person."*

Dr. Cingolani, a forensic expert, also said one person could have done it:

> *"She was grabbed by the neck very violently. Bruising on the face and nose trying to silence her, but there is no other evidence of holding her down. Her left elbow shows signs she injured it when she fell down onto the floor. The other injuries are very small. During group violence, injuries are usually bigger and more striking. The violent grasping of her throat, neck and face rules out being held down by others. If there were three people, there would be no need to use two knives."*

Forensic Engineer Ron Hendry did an extensive analysis of the blood evidence found in the room and found zero evidence suggesting multiple attackers:

> *"The evidence does not suggest multiple attackers. Much of the room was undisturbed, including items on the desk, wall shelves, and the wall hangings. The nightstand may have been jostled, but several items were left untouched on it as well. Had Meredith been attacked by multiple individuals, investigators would have found more bloody shoeprints on the floor. More items in the room would have been disturbed. Each attacker would very likely have left multiple DNA traces and perhaps fingerprints inside the room, as Rudy did. Overall, the evidence suggests that*

Meredith encountered a strong male attacker wielding a knife, who quickly overpowered and mortally wounded her."

Steve Moore had this to say about the possibility of three attackers:

"Meredith's room would have been filled with the bloody footprints, handprints, and smears of THREE PEOPLE, not one. In the world of homicide (and other) investigations, law enforcement officials and prosecutors use the word 'transfer.' Transfer is what it sounds like: the transfer of physical evidence from one person to another. Transfer is especially prevalent in murders (especially by stabbing) and rape. The nature of this case indicates that it would have the MOST transfer of any type of case. Two thirds of the required evidence missing means that two thirds of the people were not there."

Several experts testified that the knife wounds found on Meredith's body do not prove the presence of multiple attackers. The court simply overruled the experts and concluded that Meredith was killed by a trio of attackers. This conclusion goes against the evidence and lacks basic common sense.

Time of death

Evidence shows that Meredith was attacked shortly after arriving home on the night of November 1, between 9 and 9:30 pm. As we will see, the court needed to move the attack to a later time in order for their theory to fit. The court suggested that Meredith was murdered around 11:30 pm. In order to prove a later time of death, the court once again took common sense and turned it on its head.

Meredith's last meal would play a major role in determining her time of death. In his book *Unnatural Death,* Dr. Michael Baden discusses digestion of food in relation to time of death. This information is crucial to this case.

Dr. Baden makes it clear that very little interferes with the law of the digestive process. Baden states that while not accurate to the minute, the time of death can be narrowed down within two hours by examining stomach contents. The human body stops digesting food at the time of death. Baden states in his book:

"It is as elemental as rigor mortis. The digestive process stops at death."

The contents of Meredith's stomach had not yet emptied into her duodenum (the first part of the small intestine) at the time of her death. Meredith's friends testified that she ate pizza for dinner at around 6 pm, finishing up around 7 pm. Meredith then ate an apple crumble dessert at around

8 pm. The autopsy revealed undigested pizza in Meredith's stomach. Based on expert testimony regarding digestion, Meredith was murdered between 9 and 10 pm. Based on Dr. Baden's expert opinion regarding digestion, she died closer to 9 pm.

Dr. Lalli, the coroner that performed the autopsy, specified that Meredith died not more than two to three hours after eating. The court alleged that Dr. Lalli failed to conduct the autopsy properly. This was just another attempt to sabotage any evidence that contradicted the court's theory.

Thankfully the autopsy was recorded. The court watched the actual autopsy video on November 11, 2009. The video clearly showed that Dr. Lalli did everything properly including closing the duodenum to prevent slippage of the stomach contents, therefore preserving valuable evidence for proper testing.

A piece of food was found in the lower region of Meredith's esophagus. The prosecution believes Meredith ate a mushroom after returning home. This item of food was preserved by the prosecution's experts but never tested to determine what it was, which was likely a piece of apple from the apple crumble dessert she ate after dinner— not a mushroom from her home. It is no surprise that the prosecution didn't attempt to properly identify this food item. Undigested apple from Meredith's dessert would confirm the theory that the time of death was much earlier than the prosecutor was aiming for.

Meredith's phone records on the night of her murder supported the estimated time of death determined by her last meal. Meredith's phone records indicated that she normally sent a large number of text messages daily. On the evening of her murder there was very little phone activity observed on Meredith's phone. Why did Meredith decide not to send any texts that night? Her phone usage was drastically different than normal.

Meredith's friend Sophie Purton testified that Meredith arrived home shortly before 9 pm. Meredith attempted to call her mother at 8:56 pm, but the call was interrupted. If Meredith had been inadvertently cut off, it would be logical to think that she would have attempted to call again. Meredith usually spoke to her family before going to bed, as well as several times throughout the day. It is highly unlikely that Meredith would have opted out of trying to place her call again.

Three other calls were registered to Meredith's phone that night. The court suggests that Meredith was lying on her bed playing with her phone. The first call was an unsuccessful call to her voice mail. Why would Meredith have interrupted that call before hearing the voice messages? If Meredith had connected with the voice mail message even partially, the call would have appeared on the cell phone records, yet it appears nowhere except within the phone's internal memory. The call was made and stopped almost instantaneously.

The second call in question was made at 10 pm. This call was an unsuccessful attempt to call Meredith's bank.

This call was unsuccessful because it was made without the proper international prefix. Meredith knew perfectly well that she'd need to dial the proper prefix to place a call to England. There's no logical reason to believe that on this particular night, Meredith would have forgotten how to call England.

The third call in question was made at 10:13 pm. This call was recorded as a GPRS connection (reception of mms or connection to the Internet or involuntary movement). This call lasted nine seconds and was detected by a cell tower that covers the cottage as well as the location where the cell phones were found in the garden.

The court suggested that Meredith made these calls. We are supposed to believe that for no explicable reason, Meredith abandoned her normal routine of talking to her family and sending text messages to friends and instead decided to play with her phone like a child. This is absurd. Meredith knew how to call home, check her voice mail, and interact with her bank. To suggest otherwise is laughable. Meredith did not make those calls. The calls were made by Meredith's attacker.

Meredith's cell phone activity and the estimated time of death based on digestion obviously suggest that Meredith was murdered shortly after arriving home. There are additional factors to suggest this is true.

First, Meredith was still wearing her light blue Adidas jacket when she was attacked. This probably indicates that she had just arrived home and had not yet removed it. The jacket was found soaked in blood with the sleeves pulled inside out, suggesting it was forcefully removed from her body during the attack. The fact that Meredith was attacked wearing her jacket strongly suggests that she was killed shortly after arriving home.

Second, Meredith had put a load of laundry in the washer that afternoon before she had gone to her friend's house for the evening. The cottage was not equipped with a dryer. There were clothes racks in the hall where residents hung their clothes to dry. Wet laundry was found in the washer the day that Meredith's body was discovered. If Meredith had been home for two and a half hours the night before, as suggested by the prosecution, it would be logical to assume that she would have emptied the washer and hung up her clothes.

Why did the prosecution try to discredit the coroner, and why did the court feel the need to come up with a ridiculous theory to justify Meredith's phone activity? The answer is simple. Amanda and Raffaele had an alibi at the coroner's suggested time of death. Meredith's phone activity supports the coroner's report.

Raffaele was at home when Meredith was murdered. Raffaele was actively using his computer in his apartment at 9:10 pm as noted by the court. The defense also stated that computer activity showed Raffaele was active on his computer at 9:26 pm. An alibi for Raffaele is an alibi for Amanda and vice versa.

The fact that Amanda and Raffaele spent the evening alone posed a problem for them when trying to provide an alibi. Of course the same was true for anyone else in Perugia that was home alone or in the company of only one other person on the night of the murder. However, the computer activity on Raffaele's computer confirms their alibi.

The prosecution and the court chose to ignore the testimony of the people whose car stalled in front of the cottage. A man, woman, and child were in front of the cottage from 10:30 to 11:40 pm. A tow truck driver arrived at around 11:20 pm to service the vehicle. None of these witnesses saw any activity at the cottage. They all had a perfect view during the time the prosecution and the court stated the murder was taking place. Why didn't they see anyone come or go? Why didn't they witness anything unusual at all? Once again, the answer is simple. The vehicle stalled at 10:30 pm. Rudy had already committed the murder and fled the scene. The court completely ignored this testimony in the motivation. Massei had no choice. He had no way to discredit these witnesses, so he just pretended they didn't exist.

When we conclude that there wasn't a single shred of evidence in the murder room connecting Amanda and Raffaele to this horrible crime, common sense tells us they were not there. When we see that the court had to completely ignore witness testimony, ignore Meredith's phone activity, and attempt to discredit the coroner to even come close to giving their theory miniscule credibility, common sense informs us that Amanda and Raffaele had absolutely nothing to do with this crime.

Sad Reality

By now you've most likely heard the story of Pat Tilman, an army ranger killed while serving in Afghanistan. It was originally reported that he was killed by enemy fire during fierce combat. We later found out that Tilman was killed as a result of friendly fire. Army commanders along with the United States government allegedly misreported the facts surrounding Tilman's death to boost public support for the war. Regardless of their motive, the fact that Tilman's death was misrepresented was completely unacceptable and was an embarrassment to the United States military. I personally believe the military was not necessarily trying to gain positive support for the war, but was more likely doing damage control to hang onto the support they already had. Negative feelings naturally follow from hearing that one of our own soldiers has been killed by friendly fire. People simply don't want to believe that one of America's beloved heroes could die in such a way. Friendly fire is a topic that many feel uncomfortable discussing and one that leaves many with a very uneasy feeling. Unfortunately, friendly fire is one of the realities of war.

The same can be said about law enforcement. Laws are put into place to protect the masses. Bad guys are rounded up and put away so they are no longer a threat to society. Unfortunately, as with anything human beings partake in, errors occur and innocent people sometimes fall victim to wrongful accusations. It is not that police want to lock up innocent people—that is far from the truth. But authorities in any society are only human, and mistakes are bound to happen. In essence, those who are wrongly convicted are often victims of "friendly fire."

When mistakes are admitted and errors are corrected, these mistakes can be forgiven. Unfortunately there is a much darker side to wrongful convictions. Though a vast majority of those who dedicate their lives to law enforcement are good, honest human beings, there is a small percentage who are bad seeds. You will find people like this in every facet of life. It is simply unavoidable.

The sad reality is some wrongful convictions occur due to the actions of corrupt individuals. This is exactly what happened to Amanda and Raffaele.

In this chapter I will discuss a small sample of wrongful convictions. All cases are unique, but you will see similarities throughout. We must accept that wrongful convictions are a fact of life. This topic needs far more attention than it receives. We tend to brush off topics that make us feel uncomfortable. This is a problem that we must address no matter how uncomfortable it is. We never know when we may find ourselves in the same situation. Knowledge is the key to solving problems. If more people become aware of the facts regarding wrongful convictions, steps can be taken to help prevent them in the future.

Nancy DePriest was raped and murdered in Austin, Texas, in 1988. Nancy was a manager of a Pizza Hut and was attacked inside the restaurant. It seemed authorities wouldn't need to look far to find their suspects.

Christopher Ochoa and his friend Richard Danziger decided to take a look at the crime scene. They both worked at another Pizza Hut, so their curiosity wasn't out of the ordinary. Detective Hector Polanco saw it differently. He was suspicious of their behavior and wondered why they came to the restaurant to ask questions. Both were taken to the station for questioning. There was absolutely nothing wrong with Detective

Polanco's taking them in. In fact, up to that point, it was good police work. Unfortunately the actions of Polanco shortly thereafter were far from honorable and led to the wrongful conviction of two innocent men.

Christopher Ochoa was subjected to an all day interrogation by Polanco that included intimidating threats and harsh language. Ochoa was repeatedly threatened with the death penalty if he didn't confess. Polanco even described for Ochoa how the needle would go into his arm delivering the fatal injection.

This interrogation took place on a Friday. The police put Ochoa in a hotel for the weekend, shielding him from any outside contact. Ochoa was told it was for his own protection. This gave police time to prepare a confession for Ochoa to sign. Well, they didn't actually have to prepare anything. Ochoa was presented with the same confession that Polanco had used on two previous suspects. It turned out those suspects had solid alibis, so Polanco simply whited out their names on the confession and added Ochoa's. It appears that the urgency to make an arrest in the case was far more important than finding the truth.

After another long interrogation, faced with the death penalty if he didn't agree to the terms set by the authorities, Ochoa signed the confession. When later given a public defender, Ochoa was advised to agree to a plea bargain by which he would testify against Richard Danziger. Ochoa saw this plea bargain as the only way to spare his life. Ochoa and Danziger were both convicted and received life sentences. Ochoa was twenty-two at the time; Danziger was eighteen.

Years later the actual killer, Achim Marino, found religion while serving time for other offenses. Marino decided it was time to set the record straight and confess to the crime. He sent letters to the Governor's office as well as the district attorney of Texas. His letters were ignored, prompting him to write another letter giving a detailed description of the crime scene. This letter reopened the investigation. Christopher Ochoa and Richard Danziger were exonerated in 2002.

This case is a prime example of the damage caused by coerced confessions. We repeatedly find that coerced confessions do not provide accurate information, yet these tactics continue to be implemented.

Riley Fox was sexually assaulted, bound with duct tape, and drowned in a creek in Wilmington, Illinois. She was three years old at the time of her death. Months went by with no breaks in the case. Suspicion hung over her family as time went by. The media played a role in this suspicion. Amy Jacobson reported on the case for Channel 5 News in Chicago. In her report, she gave credibility to the rumors that were spreading throughout the community. Riley's parents were being watched very closely during this time. They were observed taking two vacations and purchasing a new vehicle. Rumors spread that they were spending money donated to help find Riley's killer.

None of the rumors turned out to be true. The two trips were taken to attend weddings that had been planned and paid for long before Riley was murdered. Riley's mom, Melissa, had traded in her car because she couldn't bear how it reminded her of Riley. But by the time the truth was reported, it was too late: the damage had been done. Jacobson would later say that she regretted running the story, but the station insisted that it be aired.

After five months had passed, Riley's father, Kevin, was brought in for questioning. After an all-night interrogation, he confessed to the crime. He would quickly retract his confession, but it was too late. The details of his interrogation are disturbing. According to an article in *Chicago* magazine, the interrogator told Fox that he knew people at the jail, and would make sure that Kevin was "fucked" every day unless he told them what they wanted to hear. Fox was shown pictures of his dead daughter. The interrogator told Fox, "Riley is in the room with you right now; she is in pain and needs closure."

Fox was told that the State's Attorney was offering a deal. He was told he could admit to the crime but say that it was an accident. He could take the deal or spend the rest of his life in prison. He was told the sentence would be three to five years and he would be out in half of that time. At that point Fox had been up over twenty-four hours and had been subjected to over twelve hours of questioning. He was exhausted and could no longer continue. He figured if he took the deal and ended the interrogation, he would be able to get out of that room and set the record straight. This is not uncommon after long interrogations. Many innocent people have signed confessions due to severe exhaustion. Of course, Fox was lied to: there was never any deal coming from the State's Attorney. Fox was facing first-degree murder with the possibility of the death penalty.

Many believe that the State's Attorney played a role in the arrest of Kevin Fox. Jeffery Tomczak was in a heated battle for re-election and solving this case would bring him much-needed press. Tomczak claimed that politics played no role in Fox's arrest. Nothing was ever proven, but many continue to remain suspicious of Tomczak. In my opinion, his true character was shown when he attempted to smear Fox's reputation in the press with a campaign of misinformation. Apparently voters weren't too fond of Tomczak either because he lost his re-election bid.

As Fox sat in prison, the investigation of Riley's murder continued. DNA testing ruled out Fox. With no solid evidence linking Fox to the crime, the new State's Attorney was faced with going to trial based solely on the signed confession or releasing Fox. Fox was released eight months after he was taken into custody. Not only did he lose his daughter, he now had to deal with many people who believed in his guilt. This is a natural consequence of a wrongful accusation. Many will forever believe the accusation no matter what information to the contrary.

I know this case differs from the others because Fox
was wrongly accused and not convicted, but this case
stands out to me because I felt at the time that Kevin Fox
was guilty. I listened to the news reports and was
disgusted by the crime and wanted to see justice done. I
regret to say that I was far less open-minded at the time.

The man responsible for this horrible crime is now in
custody. I hope the Fox family will be able to find some
closure. In November 2010, Scott Eby pleaded guilty to
the sexual assault and murder of three-year-old Riley
Fox.

**Deborah Sepulveda and her children, ages two and
three, together with Rose Marie Rodriguez and her
three-year-old son** were found murdered in a home in
Chicago Illinois, in 1988. The victims had been
suffocated and set on fire.

Police brought Ronald Kitchen in for questioning
based on a false tip from a jailhouse informant, Willie
Williams. Williams was looking to make a deal in hopes
of a shorter prison sentence. He later admitted that he lied
about the tip implicating Kitchen, but it was too late to
correct the damage that he caused.

Kitchen was interrogated for sixteen hours. He was
deprived of food and sleep while detectives beat him with
their fists, a phone book, and a telephone receiver. He
was also repeatedly struck in the genitals with a
nightstick. These detectives were working under
Commander Jon Burge. Burge has a history of torturing

suspects in order to extract confessions. It is reported that Burge obtained confessions by using torture methods such as suffocation, beating with various instruments, and administering electric shock to genitals. Burge was convicted in June 2010 of federal perjury and obstruction of justice for lying about the torture.

Kitchen had absolutely nothing to do with the murders. His conviction was based primarily on his confession. During his confession, Kitchen implicated another man, Marvin Reeves. Like Kitchen, Reeves was completely innocent. Confessions obtained using torture will not provide accurate information. If a person's genitals are repeatedly struck with a nightstick, they will say just about anything to get the pain to stop.

Kitchen and Reeves were fully exonerated and freed July 7, 2009. They both lost twenty-one years of their lives due to a corrupt police commander and the actions of his department.

During Kitchen's incarceration, his brother and other relatives died and his mother came down with dementia. She will never even know that her son was exonerated and freed. Kitchen also missed out on his son's childhood.

Kelly Michaels spent seven years of her life in prison for a crime she didn't commit. She was twenty-three years old at the time of her arrest. In this case there were no actual victims of any crime. The only victim was Kelly Michaels. Michaels worked at a daycare center in New

Jersey. Her nightmare began when one of the children from her daycare class made a visit to his doctor. The doctor was taking the boy's temperature rectally and the boy told the doctor that his teacher did it the same way. The doctor was suspicious as to why a teacher, in this case Michaels, would take a child's temperature rectally at school. The doctor's suspicion led to a criminal investigation.

Investigators interviewed the children at the daycare center who ranged from three to four years of age. The tactics investigators used on these children was beyond disturbing. Investigators made suggestions to the children that they had been sexually molested. These children were coached to say what the investigators wanted to hear. Children who at first repeatedly denied they were abused eventually changed their stories and said that they had been. It is very common for children to try hard to find answers that please adults. Some of the answers given indicated that the children were not being truthful. They were simply trying to give the *right* answer. One child said that Michaels played the piano naked in class, another said that "she put a sword in my rectum," and another made the wild claim that Michaels "made us eat boiled babies." After the investigation was finished, horrendous claims of abuse were announced. Michaels was accused of violating the children sexually using forks and knives, forcing them to perform sexual acts on her, and forcing them to eat feces and drink urine.

As would be expected, there was overwhelming support for the children. Our society rightfully despises wrongdoing to children. The accusations were so vile that any decent human being would demand swift justice. Parents wore shirts and buttons to court saying, "Believe the Children." The media made Michaels out to be an evil creature that preyed on innocent children.

Even though Michaels had strongly professed her innocence and also passed a polygraph, she didn't stand a chance. Michaels was convicted in August, 1988, of 115 counts of sexual abuse against twenty children and was sentenced to 47 years in prison.

In the eyes of the public, justice was served. The problem was, Michaels hadn't committed a crime. The children were not victims of sexual abuse. The entire case was fabricated by investigators based on a doctor's cautious inquiry. The children became the victims of the investigation. They were subjected to graphic details of abuse that no child should ever have to deal with.

The truth would eventually prevail. Michaels was released in 1993 after a successful appeal. The appellate court ruled that she hadn't received a fair trial. She would spend another year and a half awaiting the prosecutors' decision on whether to retry her. When they declined, all charges were dropped and Michaels was fully exonerated.

Trisha Meili was raped and beaten in New York City's Central Park on April 19, 1989. This was a horrendous crime that left Meili in a coma. Doctors feared she wouldn't survive the attack, but Meili was a fighter and made a remarkable recovery. Due to the severity of the assault, Meili has no recollection of the attack or her attacker.

Antron McCray, Kevin Richardson, Yusef Salaam, Raymond Santana, and Korey Wise were between the ages of fourteen and sixteen at the time of their arrests. During long interrogations, each of the five was told that the others had implicated him and put under extreme pressure to confess. Many false or coerced confessions come from young suspects. The pressure of the situation is often too much to bear. Four would eventually give videotaped confessions stating they committed the crime. Yusef Salaam made verbal admissions but refused to sign a confession. Korey Wise was the oldest of the group and was the only one charged as an adult.

Within weeks the four that confessed had retracted their statements, stating they were coerced. The confessions were videotaped but the long interrogations were not. The court was shown only the result of the lengthy interrogations, not the footage leading up to it. There were also many contradictions among the boys' stories. This should have been an immediate red flag. The boys differed on many major aspects of the crime including who initiated the attack, what weapons were used, and who committed the rape. These boys were telling completely different stories regarding the same crime, yet their inconsistencies were ignored.

The evidence collected at the crime scene was also ignored. DNA collected did not match any of the suspects. Even more appalling was the fact that the DNA collected all came from a single person. The evidence was telling investigators that one person committed the crime, but they refused to acknowledge it. The confessions were all that seemed to matter. All five boys were convicted.

In 2002, Matias Reyes, a convicted murderer and rapist, confessed to the crime and said he acted alone. DNA tests confirmed that Reyes committed the crime. The five boys who were wrongly convicted were exonerated. The four who were tried as juveniles had already served their entire six-year sentences. Korey Wise had served nearly twelve years in prison before he was exonerated.

Michelle Moore-Bosko was raped and murdered in 1997 in Norfolk, Virginia. Michelle was the wife of William Bosko of the United States Navy.

Five men were convicted of the crime. Four of these men, Derek Tice, Danial Williams, Joseph J. Dick Jr., and Eric C. Wilson, were wrongly convicted. Tice, Williams, and Dick were convicted of murder and were sentenced to life in prison without parole. Wilson was convicted of rape and served 8 1/2 years in prison. All four men were serving in the U.S. Navy at the time of their arrests. These men have become known as the Norfolk Four.

Omar Ballard was the fifth man convicted. All evidence suggests that he is solely responsible for this crime. He is the only man whose DNA was found at the crime scene. Forensic evidence led to only one attacker. Ballard confessed that he committed the crime alone and that no one else was involved. He continues to stand by those statements.

The convictions of the Norfolk Four were secured using confessions made by the men. All four claim their confessions were coerced, stating they were threatened with the death penalty if they did not confess. The lead detective in charge of the interrogations had a history of extracting false confessions from suspects.

Veteran FBI agent Larry Smith reviewed the case and realized that the conviction of the Norfolk Four was a miscarriage of justice. Smith saw glaring discrepancies between the confessions and the actual evidence provided at the crime scene. In an article in *Time* magazine, Smith is quoted as saying:

> *"The confession should not be the end of the investigation; you should corroborate the facts and circumstances of the confessions with the crime scene."*

Smith along with twenty-five other former FBI agents investigated the case and concluded the evidence points directly to one man, Omar Ballard. The autopsy report suggested a single attacker, and Ballard left incriminating biological evidence at the crime scene.

Smith and the other agents took interest in the case after another former agent, Frank Stokes, determined the case was a miscarriage of justice. Stokes had asked one of the case lawyers to seek the assistance of the other agents. These agents worked together to draft a letter to be sent to Governor Kaine of Virginia.

The Innocence Project had previously sent a petition for clemency to then-governor Mark Warner. That Petition would have made its way to Kaine's desk when he took over the office.

After reviewing the information presented to his office, Governor Timothy Kaine granted conditional pardons to Joseph J. Dick, Jr., Derek E. Tice, and Danial J. Williams. Kaine did not grant absolute pardons based on innocence. Eric C. Wilson had already served his full term for his rape conviction. His clemency request was denied by Governor Kaine. The four men are now free men but are still battling to clear their names. It is unfortunate that Governor Kaine fell short of completely correcting this injustice.

Retired Detective Robert Glenn Ford was convicted in October of 2010 on unrelated extortion charges of accepting payments from criminal suspects in return for favorable treatment. Ford is a perfect example of a bad seed. It is people like Ford that must be stopped. Ford should have been reassigned or fired for past wrongdoing long before he had the opportunity to interrogate the

Norfolk Four. Some positions of power should not come with second chances.

The Norfolk Four will never truly be free until they are fully exonerated. This must be done promptly so these men can move on with their lives.

I commend the efforts of the retired FBI agents that worked to correct this injustice. Veteran FBI agent Steve Moore is currently involved in a very similar effort to correct the injustice committed against Amanda Knox and Raffaele Sollecito. It is people like Larry Smith, Frank Stokes, and Steve Moore that truly make the world a better place.

Seymour and Arlene Tankleff were murdered in their home in Long Island, New York. Their seventeen-year-old son, Martin (Marty), was convicted of their murders in a highly publicized trial.

On September 7, 1988, Marty Tankleff discovered the beaten and stabbed bodies of his mother and father in their home. Marty's father was still showing signs of life. Marty immediately called 911. The operator told Marty to elevate his father's feet and apply pressure to his neck wound.

When the police arrived, Marty ran outside yelling that someone had killed his parents. Marty frantically told the police who he thought committed the crime. Marty suspected that his father's business partner, Jerry Steuerman, had attacked his parents. Seymour Tankleff's partner owed him a half a million dollars and had recently violently threatened Seymour and Arlene. It wasn't surprising that Marty suspected him.

When police entered the home they found pillows under Seymour Tankleff's feet and a white towel on his neck. Marty had done what the 911 operator told him to do. Marty tried to save his father's life. The police saw things differently. Marty had blood on his hands and he had two black eyes when police first made visual contact with him. His appearance caused immediate suspicion. The truth is that when Marty tried to save his father he got blood on his hands, and recent nasal surgery had left Marty's eyes black and blue. These details were apparently not discussed at the scene. Marty's appearance was enough to lead police to bring him in for questioning.

Marty was subjected to a brutal interrogation while experiencing grief and shock over the death of his parents. During his time of deep sorrow, investigators worked to convince Marty that he killed his parents during a blackout. Investigators lied to Marty when they told him that his father came out of his coma briefly to tell the police that he and his wife were attacked by their own son. After a long, drawn-out interrogation, Marty would eventually confess, but then he quickly recanted. The fact that Marty recanted his confession was ignored. On September 7, 1988, Marty Tankleff was convicted of murdering his parents.

Marty's conviction was secured based solely on his confession. There was no evidence at the crime scene that pointed to him. The evidence suggested a violent struggle, yet Marty didn't have a scratch on him. The details of his confession were not supported by the evidence at the scene. Marty confessed that he used a dumbbell to beat his parents. When the dumbbell was analyzed there was no sign that it had been used in the attack. The wounds were also not consistent with that type of weapon.

Hair consistent with a hair weave was found at the scene. Jerry Steuerman wore a weave. Steuerman was also the last to leave the house after the previous night's poker game. Even though Steuerman was the last person to be with Seymour Tankleff, the police never properly investigated him, instead focusing all of their attention on Marty.

Even after his conviction, many believed that Marty was innocent. Marty received a great deal of support from many people, including thirty-one former prosecutors, Barry Scheck of the Innocence Project, and The National Association of Criminal Defense Lawyers. Several TV programs highlighted the case, leading millions to conclude that Marty was innocent.

On December 21, 2007, an appellate court vacated Marty's conviction, granting him a new trial. In June of 2008, Attorney General Cuomo announced that they would not retry Marty. In July of 2008, all charges were dismissed.

Marilyn Green and her fiancé, Terry Hilliard, were gunned down in Chicago, Illinois, at the Washington Park swimming pool on the south side of the city. They were only teenagers at the time of their death.

Twenty-seven-year-old reputed gang member Anthony Porter was stopped by police as he was leaving the park that day. The police did not see anything suspicious so they let him go. Porter was charged with the crime two days later after police obtained witness testimony from another man who was also at the park that day. William Taylor was questioned at the scene and initially told police that he didn't see who committed the crime. Taylor was brought into the station and, after seventeen hours of questioning, he told a different story. Taylor's final statement said he saw Porter shoot the two victims. In this case, police obtained inaccurate information from a witness after a lengthy interrogation.

Anthony Porter was convicted and sentenced to death. He would never waiver on his claims of innocence. The testimony given by William Taylor held up in every appeal. Porter was out of options. His lawyer made one last argument that Porter did not have the mental capacity to understand his punishment of death. He argued that Porter had a low IQ and was considered mildly retarded. This argument got the attention of the *Chicago Tribune* and Cardinal George. The *Tribune* ran an editorial and Cardinal George sent a letter to the Illinois Governor to warn against "tarnishing the good name of Illinois." Just 50 hours before Porter was due to be executed, the courts granted a stay of execution.

Professor David Protess and a group of journalism students from Northwestern University, along with the volunteer help of private investigator Paul Ciolino, decided to look into the case. This small group of individuals was able to save a life and see to it that justice was served.

In a few weeks time, this volunteer group obtained a signed affidavit and videotaped statement from a woman named Inez Jackson. Jackson admitted that her husband, Alstory Simon, had committed the murders. In February 1999, Ciolino obtained a videotaped confession from Simon. Simon pled guilty in September 1999, and was sentenced to 37 years in prison.

Anthony Porter became the 76th death row inmate to be exonerated in the United States. This is unacceptable. How many others were put to death that didn't have the support Porter did? Thankfully for Porter, many people came together to fight for his freedom. Others are not so fortunate. It is important to remember that this entire ordeal stemmed from a seventeen-hour interrogation of a witness leading to false information.

Steven Branch, Christopher Byers, and Michael Moore were brutally murdered in West Memphis, Arkansas. Their bodies were found naked and bound in a drainage ditch. All three victims were only eight years old at the time of their death. This was a shockingly gruesome attack on three innocent children.

Evidence indicated that Stevie and Michael were both beaten and drowned. Christopher's death appeared to have been far more violent. He suffered violent injuries to his head and genital mutilation. Healed wounds were discovered during autopsy that suggested child abuse. Defensive wounds were found that had already healed along with fresh marks on his behind that appeared to have been inflicted with a belt.

Damien Echols, Jason Baldwin, and Jessie Misskelley have become known as the West Memphis Three. The three were teenagers at the time of their arrest in 1993 for the murder of the three boys. The circumstances of their arrest along with the investigation that was conducted cast doubt on their guilt very early on.

The crime scene was poorly handled causing potentially valuable evidence to be destroyed. The time of death couldn't be properly determined because the bodies were removed from the scene before the coroner arrived. Facts of the case were immediately released to the press causing rumors and erroneous information to quickly spread throughout the community. Due to the brutal nature of the crime, there was intense pressure to solve the crime quickly. Damien Echols was brought to the attention of authorities by Crittenden County juvenile officer Jerry Driver. Driver had somehow determined that Echols was a violent person from past interactions with him. Driver also believed that Echols was the leader of a satanic cult. There was never any evidence that the cult existed. Echols strongly proclaimed his innocence. With nothing to go on, the police questioned anyone that had ever come in contact with Echols.

Jessie Misskelley was brought in for questioning based on a tip that he had been seen with Echols. Jessie was seventeen at the time of his questioning. Arkansas law states that anyone under the age of eighteen must not be questioned without the express written consent of a parent or guardian. However, consent wasn't given by Jessie Misskelley, Sr. Jessie is mentally handicapped with an IQ of 72 and a severely diminished reading capacity. He should never have been questioned alone without the knowledge of his caretakers. After twelve hours of intense pressure and coaching, he told police he'd seen Damien Echols and Jason Baldwin attack the three boys. Jessie was no match for the seasoned interrogators and was heavily influenced by their demands for information. His answers clearly showed that he was simply doing what he could to appease the authorities. Jessie's answers contradicted the actual evidence. He told police the three victims had skipped school the day of the murders and that the attack occurred at noon. He said that Damien and Jason raped and murdered the victims and tied their bodies with rope.

Once again, false confessions do not lead to accurate information. School records proved that all three had attended school that day, so not only did they not skip school, but they were in class at noon. The medical examiner found no evidence of rape, and the boys were not bound with rope but were tied using their own shoestrings.

Only twenty minutes of the twelve-hour interrogation was recorded. As soon as Jessie realized he wasn't going home he recanted his entire testimony.

On June 3, 1993, the authorities had Damien Echols, Jason Baldwin, and Jessie Misskelley in custody based on a coerced confession. Jessie went to trial January 19, 1994. In just over two weeks he was convicted of three counts of capital murder and sentenced to life without parole.

On February 22, the trial of Jason Baldwin and Damien Echols began. Both were found guilty on March 18, with Jason being sentenced to life plus forty years and Damien sentenced to death.

Unlike the other cases that I have discussed, this injustice has not been corrected. All three of these men continue to fight for their freedom. New technology is now available that must not be ignored. DNA testing has come a long way in seventeen years. There is now definitive proof that Damien, Jason, and Jessie had nothing to do with this crime. There is not one cell of genetic material that matches any of them at the crime scene. The violent nature of the crime suggests that anyone involved would have certainly left evidence behind.

I believe Christopher Byers' stepfather, John Mark Byers is a possible suspect. I cannot say whether John Mark Byers had anything to do with the crime, but it appears to me that he was not investigated properly. Bite marks were found on the victims' bodies. Dental impressions were taken from Damien, Jason, and Jessie and they were not a match. The information regarding the bite mark evidence was released to the public letting anyone involved know the evidence existed.

Take it for what you will, but John Mark Byers had all of his teeth removed. To this day he has never given a solid explanation for this action. At one point he claimed that he lost his teeth in a fight; another time he suggested that a bad reaction to medication caused them to fall out. If I lost all of my teeth I would certainly know why.

John Mark Byers was also found to be in possession of a knife that had human blood on the blade matching Christopher Byers' blood type. An exact match could not be established. In addition, Byers' wife, Melissa Byers, died mysteriously. Her death certificate states the cause of death as undetermined.

Evidence at the crime scene, although circumstantial, also casts suspicion on John Mark Byers. Christopher's injuries were more violent than the other boys. His body showed signs of previous abuse. It appeared that more aggression was aimed at Christopher during the attack. John Mark Byers admitted at trial to striking Christopher with a belt as a form of punishment in the past.

Another possible suspect is Terry Hobbs. A hair found tied in the knots used to bind one of the victims may belong to Hobbs.

Another possible suspect is a black man that was sighted at a restaurant not far from the crime scene covered in blood and mud. The suspect became known as Mr. Bojangles, named after the restaurant. He left the restaurant before authorities arrived.

The truth is there were several leads that should have been more thoroughly pursued. Due to this negligence, this crime may never be solved.

This long, drawn-out nightmare may soon be corrected. After far too long, the state Supreme Court of Arkansas ordered new evidentiary hearings for the case in November 2010 based on DNA evidence that was unavailable during the first trial. I am confident that the court will review this evidence and Damien, Jason, and Jessie will eventually be fully exonerated. Nothing can bring back the years they have lost. Unfortunately, the damage is done.

The cases that I have mentioned are of course a very small sample. These were simply cases that stood out during my research. Several hit close to home geographically so they were of greater interest to me. The sad reality is many books could be written about thousands of wrongful convictions occurring all around the world.

The facts regarding wrongful convictions in the United States alone should cause everyone to take notice. According to the National Institute of Justice (and evaluation agency of the U.S. Department of Justice), five to ten percent of those imprisoned in the United States are innocent. That means that up to 200,000 innocent people are in prison. Ninety percent of those people pled guilty. We need to better educate ourselves on coerced confessions, accepting the fact that, while counterintuitive, false confessions do happen. Law enforcement agencies need to work together and create better ways of gathering information. It has been proven time and time again that long interrogation sessions leading to false confessions do not provide accurate information. It is time to abolish this practice now. I believe this one measure of reform would help cut down on the occurrence of wrongful convictions.

We also need individuals to step up within law enforcement and speak out when they see wrongdoing. Officers should always have the means to report wrongdoing anonymously. I have no doubt that there are members of Perugia's police force that would like to speak out about the wrongdoing they witnessed but remain silent out of fear. This is my opinion, of course, but I find it highly unlikely that no one in the department saw any wrongdoing with regard to the case of Amanda and Raffaele.

I want to make it very clear that I am in no way suggesting that we should go easy on crime. I am a true believer in law enforcement. I feel that I have a realistic view of society and I know we would be in a state of complete chaos if we lived without proper laws in place.

We need to work harder to ensure that the right people pay the price for crimes committed, and we must never stop working to keep innocent people from being wrongly convicted. When mistakes occur or corrupt individuals are exposed, corrections must be made promptly.

Injustice knows no borders and occurs in every nation on earth. We need to work together with other nations to keep these unfortunate occurrences at a minimum. If Amanda and Raffaele had been wrongly convicted in the United States, it would have been the Americans' job to stand up and see to it that Raffaele was fully exonerated and free to return home to his family. Our actions shouldn't differ depending on where an injustice takes place. Unfortunately, pride often takes over. America and Italy are rightfully proud nations and the citizens of both will stand up to defend their own people without hesitation. I am very proud of my country and I am not shy about expressing my feelings in that regard. But sometimes pride can affect our best intentions. It is easy to shout "Free Amanda" because she is an American and we want to protect her. We don't want any harm done to fellow Americans when visiting foreign nations. It is just as easy for Italians to defend their courts and to tell America to back off. I know for a fact that many Americans would be telling Italy to back off if Raffaele had been wrongfully convicted in the United States.

We need to stop this behavior and look at certain aspects of the world based solely on the fact that we are human beings and we are all one when it comes to human rights. This is no small task. If we take one step at a time in the right direction we will eventually achieve this goal. If America and Italy work together to correct the injustice committed against Amanda and Raffaele, it will be a step in the right direction.

For Our Sons & Daughters

I have been asked many times why I decided to get involved with this case. After all, I've never met Amanda Knox or Raffaele Sollecito, so why have I spent so much time defending complete strangers? I have given that question a lot of thought over the past year, and those thoughts usually lead me to another question: If one of my children ended up trapped in a nightmare similar to that of Amanda and Raffaele, besides family, who would help them?

There is nothing more important to my wife and me than the wellbeing of our children. In a few short years our children will be thinking about where to attend college. Like all parents, we'll worry as they venture out into the world for the first time. It is impossible to truly grasp how I would feel if one of my children was ever wrongly accused of a crime and imprisoned in a foreign country. I imagine that I would feel helpless. It would turn my world upside down. My wife and I would most certainly do everything in our power to defend our child but there is no doubt that we would need a great deal of help and support.

I truly believe when a person has an injustice done to them, it is the responsibility of the masses to stand up for that person; for one day that person just might be you. Even worse, that person might be your son or daughter. Most people would expect parents to protect their children at all costs. That makes it even more important for others to stand up and support Amanda and Raffaele. Family can only do so much.

Aren't you forgetting about Meredith?

I am often accused by those who are convinced that Amanda and Raffaele are guilty of forgetting the real victim. The truth is if this case was handled properly by the authorities, I may never have heard of Meredith's death. It is a sad fact that murders occur every day in every nation on earth. If Rudy Guede had been arrested early on and charged with murder—as he should have been—there is a good chance the murder would have received minimal press.

I have spent the past year researching this case. Based on expert analysis from multiple sources along with photographs and the prosecution's forensic report, I now have a very good understanding of how Meredith died. I find it offensive when people tell me that I don't care about Meredith, or that I have forgotten that she is a victim. The knowledge I have obtained regarding Meredith's death is something I will never forget. I have sympathy for Meredith's family and I understand why they want this all to end.

Any family that suffers a loss as the Kerchers have deserves to see justice served. Precisely because of the wrongful convictions of Amanda and Raffaele, Rudy is going to wind up with a lesser punishment than he deserves. Because of this, the Kerchers may never find closure. This is unacceptable and unfortunately irreparable. After three years of almost total silence, Meredith's father, John Kercher, wrote an article for the *Daily Mail* discussing this case. His words describe an overwhelming frustration over this long, drawn-out court process:

> *"This appeal, like the initial court case, will drag on for months, while the dark tunnel between my family and our ability to grieve for Meredith in peace*

becomes ever longer. If Knox doesn't get the result she wants, our agony will be even more protracted: she may then take her case to Italy's Supreme Court in Rome. Put simply, our ordeal could go on for years."

John Kercher is certainly entitled to his opinion. He and his family will spend the rest of their lives dealing with the loss of Meredith. For anyone who has not experienced a similar loss, it is impossible to imagine the pain that their family feels. I think it's unfortunate that John chose the *Daily Mail* to publish his words. The *Daily Mail* has led the media witch-hunt against Amanda from day one. Amanda Knox didn't choose to be a celebrity. She has no control over the media coverage and does absolutely nothing to suggest she wants fame. As much as I understand the need for the Kercher family to find peace, it is important to understand that the court system in Italy provides two appeals and does not consider you guilty until the process is complete.

Amanda and Raffaele are not appealing their convictions to cause more pain to the Kerchers. They are innocent and long for their freedom. They have suffered greatly. They will soon spend their fourth Christmas in prison for a crime they had absolutely nothing to do with. It is impossible for anyone who hasn't been through a similar experience to imagine the pain they have endured. Try to imagine being locked in a prison cell 23 hours a day for a crime you didn't commit. I can't fathom the fear and hopelessness of that situation.

It is ludicrous to think that two innocent people should sacrifice 25 years of their lives just so others can find peace. There is only one way to end this now and that is to correct this injustice and free Amanda and Raffaele.

You are only making things worse!
Another thing I've been told is that the support Amanda receives will actually hurt her chances of being released. Two innocent people are currently sitting in prison for a crime they didn't commit, and we're all supposed to be quiet about it. Would you be silent if your son or daughter was wrongfully convicted? If your answer is no, then you should certainly not be silent now. The words of Martin Luther King Jr. still ring true today:

> *"Injustice anywhere is a threat to justice everywhere."*

We must stand up against injustice whenever it occurs. If we fail to do so, we leave the door wide open for the same unfortunate situations to occur again and again. People should always take notice when there is a blatant attempt to silence opposition. It's generally a clear sign that there is something to hide. If you have the truth on your side, there should be no fear of opposing voices. If the truth is allowed to be heard it will eventually prevail.

At the time of this writing, the appeal for Amanda and Raffaele is just getting underway. I am hopeful that the citizens of Perugia, Italy, will find the courage to stand up against this injustice. Not just for Amanda and Raffaele, but for their children and the children of future generations.

This injustice must be corrected and we must never forget how and why it occurred. Please take time to learn more about wrongful convictions. Together we can all make a difference. In doing so, we will help to make the world a better place for our sons and daughters.

Acknowledgements

There are many people to thank. The Injustice in Perugia website and this book are the result of the hard work of many people. I will do my best to include everyone and I apologize if I have left anyone out.

Jim Lovering is at the heart of the effort to free Amanda and Raffaele. Jim has access to case files and has provided me with vast amounts of information including crime scene videos, photographs and documents. I would have been unable to complete this project without this access. More importantly, Jim has provided invaluable advice to those who have come together to offer support. He is a gifted communicator and he has reminded me on more than one occasion that shouting at the opposition accomplishes very little. I am very grateful for Jim's knowledge and guidance; Mark Waterbury is a man that I have great respect for. It was his direct hard hitting articles that drew me in early on. After reading just a few paragraphs on Mark's blog, it was very clear to me that an injustice had occurred; I am grateful for my many conversations with Ray Turner. Ray tells it like it is. This case is ridiculous. It's that simple. His blog is an excellent source for information. I look forward to many more conversations with Ray in the

315

future; Christopher Halkides provides important information regarding this case on his blog. Chris does an excellent job of discussing the case with those who may not agree with him. I like his approach. When someone is shouting at you, there is no need to shout back. Just calmly let them know they are wrong and explain why with facts; Candace Dempsey was another voice of reason early on. Her blog provided one of the first forums for discussion and helped to expose many of the flaws in this case. Candace's book was the first to tell the truth about this case and will be read for many years to come; Steve and Michelle Moore have been truly inspiring. Steve's professional analysis is excellent. He has not only helped me to better understand certain aspects of this case, he has presented his analysis to the public in a very professional and respectful manner. His no nonsense approach leaves no doubt that an injustice has occurred. Steve and Michelle have sacrificed greatly to support something they believe in. They have my sincere respect. There is much more to be written about how influential Steve and Michelle have been as well as many others in our group. I have taken Steve's advice and have decided to hold off on writing about our personal experiences until a later time. Our only focus now is to free Amanda and Raffaele; Ron Hendry is a stubborn man. He knows the truth and will not waver in his opinion. He has no reason to waver because his analysis is correct. I have gained a great deal of knowledge from Ron. His analysis reveals several key points that were previously overlooked. His reconstruction of the crime scene provides invaluable information. I am grateful that Ron contacted me to offer his expertise. He is a shining example of the many people that have come together to right a wrong, looking for nothing in return. He has my utmost respect; Jason has dedicated a great deal of time to this cause all while raising a family. He has done a fantastic job collecting letters for Amanda and Raffaele. This is an extremely important task and there is no one better suited for the job. He has done far too much behind the scenes for Amanda and Raffaele to mention here. He is a good honest person that I am honored to call a friend; Sarah Snyder has done more for this cause than anyone will ever know. She has dedicated countless hours behind the scenes making things happen. Most recently Sarah has been instrumental in setting up interviews for Steve Moore and Ron Hendry. She has offered me excellent advice that I have incorporated into the website and this book. Sarah has been one of the main contributors to Injustice in Perugia. Even though she will never ask for it, she deserves a great deal of credit for her efforts; Michael Charles Becker is an excellent writer and I am hopeful he will author a book of his own some day. I have benefited from reading his perspective. Michael summed up the entire case when he gave a much more appropriate title to the Massei report. We now know it as *"the speculation report"*; Andrew Lowery has been outspoken about this case from very early on. If it wasn't for people like Andrew exposing this injustice in the beginning, I doubt the support group we have today would exist. Andrew does an excellent job running the Italian language site. He also worked with Mark Waterbury to develop a couple of the most widely viewed videos regarding this case; David Kamanski is an attorney that dedicated many hours of his time to help prepare the appeal summaries that are currently available on the Injustice in Perugia website. The appeals provided valuable information for this book. David also spends quite a bit of time on the discussion forums providing factual information to the public. He is another gifted communicator that has helped many to see the truth about this case; Joseph Bishop has been one of the most effective supporters of this cause. His comments on articles throughout the internet refute the guilter cut and paste nonsense in definitive fashion. Joseph brought the lack of transparency in the Italian justice system to my attention. I believe this is an extremely important topic. Joseph is a very charitable man. He is quick to offer airfare to members of our group, and he is present at many of the events to support Amanda's defense fund. The world needs more people like Joseph Bishop; I would like to thank Patrick for managing the Injustice in Perugia Twitter account, Steve Shay for his dedication to excellent journalism, Anne Bremner for her continued work on this case, Judge Michael Heavey for his dedication and personal sacrifice, and Douglas Preston for writing Monster of Florence.

I would also like to thank the many people that have come forward to voice their support for Amanda and Raffaele in various discussion forums. Our facebook group discussions have been very inspiring to me. I am very pleased to have the opportunity to be a part of such a great group of people. I would like to thank; Alexander, Amanda, Anna, Anthony, Catherine, Chris C., Dan O., Davelebon, Eve, Grace, Heather H., Jake, Jeff B., Joe S., Jodie, John O., HumanityBlues, Karen, Kestrel, Larry, Lisa G., Lisa R., LondonSupporter, Loretta, Mary, Michael Krom, Michael S., Mickey, Moodstream, Paul,

Rhea, Rick, Ron, Rose, Ryan, Sept79, Sherry, Shirley, Struoc and many others.

Thank you to Georgio and Maurice for their assistance with translation.

Additional thanks to Andrew Lowery for designing the cover for this book.

Photographs provided by Jim Lovering, raffaelesollecito.org, and amandadefensefund.org.

Lastly, I would like to give a very special thank you to Heather Coy. This book would have never been possible without her. She not only helped me greatly with her personal advice, she also put my mind at ease with her excellent editing skills. Heather has also dedicated a great deal of personal time to the cause. In 2010, she organized a very successful event to benefit the Amanda Knox Defense fund. She is another member of our group that has done far too much behind the scenes to mention here.

Recommended Books

Murder in Italy: The Shocking Slaying of a British Student, the Accused American Girl, and an International Scandal by Candace Dempsey

The Monster of Perugia – The Framing of Amanda Knox by Mark Waterbury

The Monster of Florence by Douglas Preston and Mario Spezi

Recommended Websites

Injustice in Perugia has a group of websites related to the case.

Injustice in Perugia (www.injusticeinperugia.org)

Italian Language Site (www.amandaknox.it)

Injustice in Perugia Member's Forum (www.injusticeinperugiaforum.org)

Injustice Blog (http://injusticeinperugia.blogspot.com)

Even though I created Injustice in Perugia, I honestly think Jim Lovering described the site best: *"This site provides detailed, up-to-date information. It is part of a wave of activism that continues to build in support of Amanda and Raffaele. This wave is spontaneous, it is not under the control of any individual or agency, and it will not subside until Amanda and Raffaele are free and exonerated of all charges."*

Andrew Lowery has done an excellent job on the Italian Language site. The site offers expert analysis from Mark Waterbury and Steve Moore and also provides the full appeal documents filed by both defense teams.

Injustice in Perugia also has a Member's Forum for those who would like to join in on the discussion. This forum is not only an excellent source of information; it also provides a positive setting for intelligent discussion for those who support Amanda and Raffaele.

Lastly, Injustice in Perugia has a blog that has minimal moderation and is open for all discussion.

Science Spheres (www.sciencespheres.org)

Mark Waterbury, Ph.D., has done extensive research regarding this case. His blog reviews the distorted and pseudoscientific evidence developed by the prosecution to justify their incarceration. Mark is also the author of The Monster of Perugia – The Framing of Amanda Knox, a book about the case.

Friends of Amanda (www.friendsofamanda.org)

This site provides detailed information about this case. Jim Lovering does an excellent job of presenting information in an easy to read format with well organized links to his sources. It was this website along with Science Spheres and Ray Turner's blog that influenced me to learn more.

Raffaele Sollecito (www.raffaelesollecito.org)

This is an excellent place to learn about the real Raffaele Sollecito. The media often ignores Raffaele even though he is suffering equally in this ordeal. Please visit this website and learn more about Raffaele.

The Ridiculous Case Against Amanda Knox and Raffaele Sollecito (http://knoxarchives.blogspot.com/)

Ray Turner's blog discuses the major flaws in the prosecution's case. Contributors Jim Lovering, Andrew Lowery and Ray Turner provide their perspective on the wide range of issues that plague the prosecution's case.

View-From-Wilmington (www.viewfromwilmington.blogspot.com)

Chris Halkides, associate professor of chemistry and biochemistry at the University of North Carolina at Wilmington, has written a series of excellent articles in regard to the case.

Italian Woman at the Table (http://blog.seattlepi.com/dempsey/index.asp)

Candace Dempsey's true crime blog offers continuing coverage on the case. Candace is also the author of Murder in Italy, a book about the case.

Innocence Project (www.innocenceproject.org)

Please visit this website to learn more about wrongful convictions. The site is an excellent resource for up to date information. Please get involved. The innocence project has helped to free hundreds of wrongfully convicted people. They are a great organization that needs your support.

You Can Help

By purchasing this book you have already made a donation to support the defense of Amanda and Raffaele. I would like to personally thank you for your purchase.

Amanda and Raffaele have both repeatedly expressed their appreciation for all of the support they receive. In November 2008, Amanda wrote an open letter to Seattle Prep to express her appreciation:

> *"I don't know if I can really express what it means to me to have the people who have known me (and even those that haven't) by my side throughout all of this... After a year I at least have learned to respond to the negativity of my current environment as peacefully and calmly as possible, but my family is still out there in the world that just can't seem to make up its mind about what to do with my life. So thank you, thank you, thank you. I'm incredibly moved by how much care the Seattle Prep community has put forth that I never expected and yet never have doubted."*

She finished her letter with the Italian phrase:

"Io lo so che non sono sola anche quando sono sola
— Even when I am alone I'm not alone"

Raffaele has written several private letters of appreciation for the support he receives.

If you are able to contribute further to Amanda and Raffaele, please visit the websites below.

www.amandadefensefund.org

www.raffaelesollecito.org

Get Involved
Please join the Injustice in Perugia Member's Forum, visit the recommended websites and read the recommended books. There are many ways to help besides making donations. Please join in the discussion and help the ongoing effort to spread the word about this injustice.